SAVING
FOR
AMERICA'S
ECONOMIC
FUTURE

SAVING
FOR
AMERICA'S ECONOMIC FUTURE

Parables & Policies

Laurence S. Seidman

M. E. Sharpe, Inc.
Armonk, New York   London, England

Copyright © 1990 by M. E. Sharpe, Inc.

Available in the United Kingdom and Europe from M. E. Sharpe,
Publishers, 3 Henrietta Street, London WC2E 8LU.

Library of Congress Cataloging-in-Publication Data

Seidman, Laurence S.
    Saving for America's economic future: parables and policies
/ by Laurence S. Seidman.
        p.   cm.
    Includes bibliographical references.
    ISBN 0-87332-578-8—ISBN 0-87332-579-6 (pbk.)
    1. United States—Economic policy—1981– I. Title.
HC106.8.S44   1989
338.973 ′009 ′048—dc20   89-24219
                                                               CIP

Printed in the United States of America

∞

BB 10 9 8 7 6 5 4 3 2 1

For my parents, Eleanor and Irving Seidman

CONTENTS

PREFACE

This is a serious book about a serious subject. But that doesn't mean that every page must contain the serious terms of formal economics. This book tries to challenge the conventional wisdom about substance: It delineates economic policies we can adopt to meet our economic challenges. But it also tries to challenge the conventional wisdom about style: It sets forth a serious analysis in a lighter vein.

Can good economics be entertaining—at least some of the time? Is it possible to learn economics while smiling—at least occasionally? Can economic policies be made interesting—at least most of the time? I believe the answer to these questions is yes. That's why I've written this book, and written it as though economics were potentially enjoyable as well as serious and important.

As we enter the 1990s, there is deep concern about our nation's economic future. Best sellers, magazine articles, and speeches ask: Will the United States decline? What can we do to stay second to none? How can we save America's economic future? How can the United States meet its economic challenges?

I try to give serious answers to these questions. But please note the cast of characters that try to make my answers more enjoyable and memorable: Adam and Eve (chaps. 1 and 8), Senator Myopia (chap. 2), emaciated S and the lazy heir (chap. 3), old Karl (chap. 6), the passionate objector (chap. 9), XT (chap. 10), President Competitus and Senator Economus (chap. 11), and the heir to Khomeini (chap. 12). Every chapter strives for a light, conversational exposition of a serious subject.

As a professor of economics, I spend most of my time writing technical articles for economics journals and teaching college students from textbooks (I've written one myself). I believe strongly that we academics, immersed in technical work, should occasionally take time out to communicate to a wider audience. After all, if we don't, there are others, whose skill at writing far surpasses their knowledge of economics, who will be glad to entertain and mislead that wider audience.

So I've tried to make this serious subject accessible and enjoyable. I hope you find it stimulating and persuasive.

For suggestions, I wish to thank Henry Aaron, Burton Abrams, Lee Anderson, Richard Agnello, Stacie Beck, David Black, Eric Brucker, James Butkiewicz, Yung-Ping Chen, Philip Cook, Eleanor Craig, Lawrence Donnelley, Robert Frank, Fred Geldon, Farley Grubb, David Haslett, Saul Hoffman, Harry Hutchinson, John Immerwahr, Robert Inman, Richard Kane, Kenneth Koford, Bertram Levin, Kenneth Lewis, Charles Link, Jeffrey Miller, Ronald Mincy, Richard Murnane, Robert Myers, George Parsons, Ann Kane Seidman, Eleanor Seidman, Irving Seidman, Leon Seidman, Robert Seidman, Jerrold Schneider, Anita Schwarz, Russell Settle, Robert Stein, James Thornton, and John Wesley. Finally, I am grateful to my daughter Suzanna, my son Jesse, and my wife Ann.

SAVING
FOR
AMERICA'S
ECONOMIC
FUTURE

1

AN ECONOMIST'S GENESIS

In the beginning, Adam and Eve had no tools. To compensate, God saw to it that the weather and soil never failed them. Initially, Adam and Eve devoted all their working time to growing food. With their bare hands, they plowed, planted, and harvested. Each year, they consumed all the food they produced, and each year, production and consumption remained the same. For all we know, Adam and Eve were happy.

Adam's dream

But one night, Adam had a dream. With an imagination that leaped centuries, Adam dreamed of a tractor. In the dream, Adam saw their ability to plow, plant, and harvest multiply.

"If only we had a tractor." The thought haunted Adam and Eve for weeks to come, as they continued to farm with their bare hands. Naturally, they prayed daily to God to give them a tractor. But to no avail.

One day, Adam and Eve were walking in the garden.

"So you want a tractor?" spoke a deep voice. And they knew the voice was God's.

"Yes," they trembled. And God answered, "Do you expect a

tractor to fall from the sky like manna from Heaven?''

And Adam and Eve whispered, ''That's exactly what we were hoping.''

Then God laughed in a kind voice, ''No, my children, it is time for you to eat from the tree of economic knowledge. I will not give you a tractor. You must make your own tractor, by the sweat of your brow.''

''That's just what we were afraid of,'' said Adam and Eve. Then, God burned detailed instructions—''How to Make a Tractor''—onto a tablet of stone that lay at the foot of the tree of economic knowledge. As they sat under the tree, eating its fruit and reading the instructions, Adam and Eve suddenly realized a fundamental truth of the human condition. They realized that, while making a tractor, they must devote less time to plowing, planting, and harvesting food. In the short run, they must reduce their consumption of food.

''We face a trade-off,'' said Eve suddenly. ''We must sacrifice consumption in the present, while we build the tractor, in order to enjoy more consumption in the future.''

''Isn't there any way around this?'' asked Adam gloomily.

''I'm afraid not,'' said Eve, who may have been the second person, but was clearly the first economist. ''No sacrifice, no rise in the standard of living. It's that simple, honey.''

Having eaten from the tree of economic knowledge, Adam and Eve decided to do their accounting properly. Although they knew it was unnecessary in their simple economy, they decided it would be fun to use money to keep track, and more importantly, to help their descendants understand the fundamentals. Conveniently, identical rectangular-shaped green leaves hung from the branches of the tree of economic knowledge. By fiat, Adam and Eve declared each leaf to be one dollar ($1). Here's how they did their accounting.

They began with the pre-tractor economy. Each year they produced a hundred units of food. They arbitrarily declared the price per unit of food to be $1, so that total output (which they also called gross national product, or GNP) was $100.

The ritual

To illustrate a basic truth of national income accounting, Adam and Eve engaged in a ritual. Playing the role of consumers, they paid $100 for the food, which they called *output*, placing the hundred leaves on a flat boulder beneath the tree of economic knowledge. Immediately, they circled to the opposite side of the boulder to play the role of producers, and promptly picked up the hundred leaves, thereby receiving $100 of *income* from the sale of the food.

"What a coincidence," said Adam. "We bought $100 of output, and also received exactly $100 of income."

With patience and sensitivity, Eve made her husband see that it had to be so. "Output equals income" whispered Eve softly. "It's our first accounting identity."

They also noted that in the pre-tractor economy, total consumption was equal to total output—$100.

Then Eve said, "Let's *assume* we built a tractor this year."

"But we didn't," Adam objected.

"I'm an economist," Eve retorted. "I can assume anything I want. Now let's redo our accounting. Assume we devoted 40 percent of our work time to the construction of one tractor. Then our time spent on food production fell 40 percent, so food output fell from a hundred to sixty units."

As good accountants, they reasoned as follows. Since the total labor time devoted to all production (food plus tractor) was the same, total output should still be valued at $100. Since output of the consumer good fell from $100 to $60, the price of the tractor should be set at $40, so that total output would remain $100.

"Let's call food the 'consumer' good," expounded Eve, "because it is used up—consumed—in the year it is produced. Let's call the tractor the 'investment' good, because it raises productive power in future years."

"I have another accounting identity," she then exclaimed. "Output ($100) equals consumption ($60) plus investment ($40)."

Then they performed their ritual at the boulder under the tree. Two goods were now available for sale: the consumer good (food), and the investment good (the tractor). Playing the role of consumers, Adam and Eve paid $60 for the food. Playing the role of investors, they paid $40 for the tractor. Immediately, they circled to the opposite side of the boulder and, as producers, promptly received $100 of income.

"Notice," said Eve, "that we consumed $40 less than our income; our income was $100, and our consumption was only $60. I propose that we *define* income minus consumption to be *saving*. Our saving, therefore, was $40."

"What a coincidence," said Adam. "Our investment was also $40."

Once again, with gentle patience, Eve tried to explain to her husband that it had to be so, that saving had to equal investment. But this time she found it harder to make him grasp the point.

Suddenly she exclaimed, "A bank! I'll show him with a bank."

Eve promptly declared a nearby boulder to be a bank. She said to Adam, "Let's do the ritual again."

But this time when, as producers, they received the $100 of income, Eve said to her husband, "Let's save $40 of our income. Let's put $40 in that bank over there."

She led Adam by the hand to the bank, and deposited the $40 on top of the bank boulder. "We've just saved $40 of our income. We'll consume the remaining $60."

"Now," she said, "let's play the role of investors who want to buy the tractor. We'll borrow $40 from the bank." At the bank boulder, she took the $40 that had been saved, and leading Adam back to the original boulder, used the $40 to buy the tractor.

"Investment equals saving," she whispered softly. "It's our third accounting identity."

Then Eve sat under the tree of economic knowledge, lost in thought. Suddenly, she jumped to her feet.

"Do you realize what this means, dear husband? Investment, unlike consumption, raises our future productive power. But to invest, we must save. And saving means consuming less than our income.''

"And there isn't any way around it?'' asked Adam once again.

"None whatsoever,'' replied Eve. "You don't get something for nothing,'' she added, her cheerful tone confirming that she was, indeed, the first economist.

Adam grumbled, "You certainly do practice a dismal science.''

Optimal saving in a lonely Eden

Adam paced anxiously under the tree of economic knowledge.

"What's the matter dear?'' asked Eve.

Adam's eyes darted in all directions.

"I don't think I want to build the tractor,'' he confessed guiltily. "Of course, I want the tractor. But I don't want to save for the tractor. I can't bear to cut my consumption,'' he blurted out, tears streaming down his face. "There, there, dear,'' Eve comforted him. "I know how much trips to our little food mall mean to you. You've become quite attached to it.''

"I'm addicted to it,'' Adam cried out in despair. "I don't think I can survive a cut in my consumption, even for one year. Eve, I need a compassionate therapist, and curse my lot, the only other living being is an economist.''

Without taking offense, Eve replied, "Now dear, I know what you've heard about economists—that they are devoid of emotion, that they depict man as a calculating robot, that all they care about are dollars and cents. But you forget that all this came later, after Adam Smith glorified the virtues of specialization. For God's sake, this is Eden, we're the only two people on Earth—at least, as far as we know—so I can't afford to be only an economist. I also have a degree in psychology. Let me help. Here, lie down on this couch, and try to relax.''

Eve's tender, soothing voice convinced Adam that she was, indeed, more than just an economist. Maybe she could help him with his overwhelming guilt. Adam lay down, without even asking where the couch came from.

"Eve," Adam confessed, "I know that economics teaches that saving is always better than consuming. I know my lust for consumption is wrong. But I can't repress it."

"Adam, this may come as a pleasant shock to you, but that is not what modern economics teaches. Saving is not always better than consuming." Adam was indeed shocked.

"I don't understand," he gasped with relief.

"Believe it or not," Eve continued, "economics cannot tell you whether to save or not. Economics simply shows you the consequence. It's then up to you to decide."

"What do you mean by 'consequence'?" Adam asked.

"Well," answered Eve, "here's how an economist would help you make your decision. First, she would ask: Once the tractor is built, how much will it raise food output in each future year?"

"In my dream," Adam replied, "the tractor raised food output $20 per year, forever."

"How convenient that God has not yet cursed mankind with depreciation," Eve laughed. "Since the tractor lasts forever—it never depreciates, or wears out—we can easily compute the 'rate of return' on our saving. The tractor will cost us $40 of consumption, but it will then yield a return of $20 per year, so the rate of return is $20 divided by $40, or 50 percent."

Agitated, Adam asked, "Doesn't economics teach that you should save if the rate of return is 50 percent?"

"No," Eve replied in a soothing voice. "Economics simply asks you to compare, in your mind, two situations. Under the first, without the tractor, you consume $100 of food in every year. Under the second, with the tractor, you consume $60 in the first year, and then $120 in all future years. Economics then says that there is no right or wrong choice. Whatever you decide is OK with economics. Just as economics does not presume to tell you whether to eat fewer apples and more oranges, so economics does not presume to tell you whether to consume less in the present, and more in the future."

"You mean, economics accepts 'consumer sovereignty' and

applies the principle to present vs. future consumption, as well as to apples vs. oranges?'' Adam asked with a feeling of relief.

"Yes,'' Eve laughed, gently wiping the perspiration off her husband's forehead with a fig leaf. "You can check any standard economics text.''

"So I can decide whatever I want, as long as I recognize the trade-off, and economics will not condemn me?'' asked Adam joyfully.

"Yes, my love,'' Eve replied.

"Oh Eve, please, can we forget the tractor? I just can't bear to cut consumption below $100, even if the return on my saving is 50 percent.''

"Move over,'' whispered Eve, and within moments the two had forgotten the tractor.

Far East of Eden

And so, Adam and Eve lived happily as though the dream had never occurred, until one day, while wandering Far East of Eden, Adam discovered a large island shaped like the letter J. One of Adam's greatest pleasures was naming things and places, so when he climbed the island's highest mountain, he exclaimed, "Let this be Mount Fuji.'' Exhilarated by the view from Fuji's summit, Adam gazed down into the valley.

"I am truly happy,'' he said to himself.

But at that very moment, Adam received a shock. Was that smoke? Could it be? Adam squinted. Were those two human forms? Adam pulled out his pocket bible and reread the first chapter. Then he squinted again, and stealthily descended the mountain to get a better look. Behind a huge rock, Adam trembled. Less than a hundred yards away was another human couple.

With fear, Adam whispered, "Let them be couple J.''

Adam eavesdropped, and what he heard struck terror into his heart. Couple J had somehow obtained tractor instructions, and was contemplating the same decision: to save or not to save. To his horror, Adam overheard the decision: couple J would save enough, not for one, but for two tractors. When darkness fell, Adam fled the island, and raced to Eden to report the news. An agitated dinner ensued.

"Why should we care what the J's do?" said Eve. "We made our decision. Let them make theirs. If they are willing to make the present sacrifice, let them enjoy a higher standard of living in the future."

As the first economist, Eve pointed out that her subjective "utility" (satisfaction) should depend only on her own (and Adam's) consumption, not on the J's consumption. In fact, she planned to write a standard economics textbook postulating that a person's utility depends only on his own consumption, not on anyone else's.

"Relativity has no place in standard economics," she insisted.

But Adam was not so sure. He said, "This may be a bad time to bring it up, my love, but do we plan to have children? Because if we do, we're going to have a problem. Our children are bound to learn about couple J's children. After all, communication and transportation are bound to improve, and the J's may even come to Eden as tourists. What will we tell our children when they discover that they consume less than J children because we sacrificed less than J parents?"

"We'll tell them," Eve replied adamantly, "that they should avoid standard of living comparisons. We'll teach them that envy is wrong. If all else fails, we'll show them that standard economics textbooks postulate that individuals are unaffected by relativity."

But even as she spoke these words, Eve began to feel uneasy. She was a good economist who had mastered the standard framework, but she retained an open mind about its assumptions.

"What if relativity does matter to our children?" she asked herself. "What if human nature cannot be purged of relativity?"

Adam continued, "There is a certain irony in the confession I'm about to make, but I've been reading some works in evolutionary biology. The argument goes like this. Suppose an individual who monitors his relative position, and adjusts his effort accordingly—intensifying it when he's falling behind, relaxing it when he's ahead—is more likely to survive when a crisis, such as famine or predator attack, occurs. If so, then a relativity emotion may be selected for by, dare I say it, a Darwinian process. We may be unable to purge our descendants of relativity. If their standard of living is worse than the J's, they will be unable to ignore it, no matter what we say."[1]

Now it was Eve's turn to be glum. "Maybe we'd better match the J's saving," she said.

That night it was Eve's turn to dream. In her dream, she envisioned herself on Mount Fuji, watching the J's below. She watched them build two tractors. How they sacrificed in the year the tractors were built. They cut their consumption to $20, saved $80, and built two tractors worth $40 each. But then Eve watched them, the next year, use the two tractors to plant, plow, and harvest. The J's and their children now enjoyed much more than $100 of consumption, and would do so forever. And the additional consumption was not simply food. Somehow, the J's were making and consuming dazzling appliances, undreamed of in Eden.

"No!" Eve cried in her dream. To Eve's horror, she saw the J's board an airplane, and travel to Eden. With them they brought their appliances, not for sale, but for show. The children of Eden were filled with awe and wonder. Why don't we have those? they asked. Eve saw an expression of sorrow come over the J's faces. They pitied the poor children of Eden.

"No!" Eve screamed, and she awoke, drenched in perspiration. "We can't let it happen," she sobbed in Adam's arms.

"Everything has changed," Adam said grimly. "Woe, that I ever set eyes on the J island."

Note

1. I owe this argument, and my emphasis on the importance of relativity, to the fascinating book by Cornell University economist Robert Frank, *Choosing the Right Pond: Human Behavior and the Quest for Status* (New York: Oxford University Press, 1985).

2

RAISE THE NATIONAL
SAVING RATE

Senator Myopia had the Mall crowd cheering. Outside, the snow fell, and a weaker people might have huddled in their homes. But undaunted, sturdy Americans had ventured out into the winter storm, lured by the warmth of the great American Mall. Now in the warm belly of the Mall, surrounded by sparkling shop windows, how glad they were that their pioneer fortitude had triumphed.

The shop windows of the great American Mall vibrated as the crowd roared its approval. Only a speaker like Senator Myopia could grab the attention of frantic Mall shoppers, and interrupt their frenzied purchases.

"I'm sick and tired of the party poopers, the kill-joys, the austerity pushers, and the discipline devotees who say we must sacrifice to stay number one. How dare they attack our most sacred institution, the great American Mall!" roared Senator Myopia.

"You know, I've traced my lineage all the way back to Ancient Greece and Rome, but my fellow Americans, let me tell you something. The Romans were great builders, but their Empire fell, and do you know why? Because they never built a great Mall. And this, my friends, is why America shall endure and thrive forever. Oh sure, we must save more. Sure, we must invest more. But first and foremost, my fellow Americans, we must consume more!'' The crowd erupted in thunderous applause.

"Let's make those cash registers hum,'' continued the senator. "The more we consume, the stronger our economy will be. Who dares to spoil our party?'' mocked the senator with sarcasm, as the crowd broke into approving laughter.

"I do,'' said a young man in the corner. The crowd hushed, and a thousand eyes turned to him. He began to speak, but Senator Myopia immediately interrupted him.

"So you'd like to spoil our party, would you?'' asked Senator Myopia with a confident grin. "And you expect us to listen to you. But just look at you. Your clothes. Who handed them down to you, your older brother, or your father?'' The crowd began to snicker.

"And there's nothing in your arms, except a single book. Where are your packages? Could it be you left your credit cards home? Or don't you even have a set of credit cards?'' The very thought of someone without credit cards sent the crowd into a fit of laughter.

But the young man seemed unruffled. In a calm voice he said: "In order to raise our saving rate, we must reduce our consumption rate. If our saving rate is 15 percent, our consumption rate is 85 percent. Raising the saving rate from 15 percent to 18 percent means reducing the consumption rate from 85 percent to 82 percent.''

Now Senator Myopia became angry. "That's the stupidest thing I've ever heard. I say we can raise both our saving rate and our consumption rate at the same time.''

"I'm afraid that's not possible, Senator,'' the young man continued. "You see, saving is defined as income minus consumption. The saving rate is the fraction of income saved, and the consumption rate is the fraction of income consumed. The two must add up to 100 percent. So if the saving rate is to go up, the consumption rate must go down. I'm afraid it's that simple.''

"Who are you?'' shouted the angry senator. "What do you do for a living?'' muttered voices in the crowd.

"I'm an economist," answered the young man in a quiet voice.

"An economist!" smirked Senator Myopia. "Did you hear that, my fellow Americans, an economist! Is this the kind of person you would invite to your house for dinner? Would you want your children around this kind of person? What do you do for fun, young man, read a textbook?" The crowd went wild with derisive laughter.

"Ignore him, Senator!" shouted the crowd. And so the senator did. He brought his oration to a dramatic crescendo.

"Consume, consume, consume, my fellow Americans. Let's go out and spend ourselves rich!" With that, the crowd cheered, and burst into the waiting shops. The senator and his party soon left, triumphant.

But in the corner, the young man remained. And he did not remain alone. Several people, young and old, quietly gathered around him, and urged him to teach them. And here is what he said.

The role of capital accumulation

I'm afraid, my friends, I've begun with a simple, unpleasant truth. A higher saving rate inescapably means a lower consumption rate. So, should we raise the saving rate? Yes, I believe there is a decisive reason for raising our saving rate: the relative standard of living of our children and grandchildren. If we do not raise our saving rate, then within a few decades, several other nations will overtake our standard of living. If we maintain our current saving rate, today we will enjoy the highest consumption per person in the world, but tomorrow our children and grandchildren will not.

Senator Myopia mocked my clothes. He accused me of not caring about consumption. But that is untrue. I do not come to preach against materialism. Far from it. I love stereos, airplane travel, and many other material things. I do not place myself above my fellow citizens who shop frantically all around us.

My difference with Senator Myopia is simply this. In his obsession with consumption today, he forgets about consumption tomorrow. He fails to grasp what we must do today to protect consumption tomorrow. He thinks the best way to achieve high consumption tomorrow is to enjoy fast consumption growth today. Unfortunately, he is wrong. So I come to plead for a higher saving rate today, not because I am against consumption, but because I am for it—in the future as well as the present. I want our future consumption to be second to none in the world.

Nor am I an extremist. I don't advocate an actual cut in our consumption, only slower consumption growth for a few years. Instead of our normal 3 percent consumption growth, let it grow 1 percent for a while. I want a small cut in our consumption *rate* (the fraction of our output that we consume) each year for several years—small enough so that our dollar consumption keeps rising each year, yet more slowly than it would otherwise.

To understand my case for gradually raising our national saving rate, you must first understand what capital accumulation is, and how it raises the standard of living (the level of consumption per person).

Let me begin with a question. What determines the rate of improvement in a nation's standard of living in the long run? Of course, many factors influence the rate of advance. But one source, my friends, deserves the spotlight: capital accumulation. What is capital accumulation? Are you thinking of stocks and bonds, those impressive pieces of paper we often lock up in a bank vault for safety? Or are you thinking of financial capital, the funds that finance the purchase of stocks and bonds? By "capital," I do not mean either the pieces of paper, or the funds that buy them. Instead, I mean *real* capital which, when combined with labor, produces real output. Capital enables the average worker to produce more output.

What do you think real capital is? Are you thinking of machines? Many people think capital consists solely of physical capital, like machines. But this view of capital is too narrow. Of course, physical capital is vital. What would our standard of living be without machinery, factories, roads, and bridges?

Where would today's farmer be without a tractor?

But capital is more than machinery. Capital is also the stock of technical knowledge accumulated from past experience. This stock of "blueprints" tells us how to produce specific goods and services. Just imagine the consequence of a national amnesia that would require us to reinvent the wheel, and everything else. Did you realize that capital is also the skill of the labor force that is acquired by education and training? The stock of blueprints and machinery are not very effective unless the work force has accumulated the human capital (skills) needed to follow the blueprints and operate the machines.

Suppose the capital stock is $2,000 billion on January 1. Suppose that during the year $500 billion of new capital goods are produced, and $300 billion of old capital goods wear out—"depreciate"—so that the capital stock is $2,200 billion on December 31. Then we say that this year's *gross investment* is $500 billion, and the *net investment* is $200 billion. So *net* investment is the net increase in the capital stock that occurs during the year—in this example, $200 billion. Given the amount of capital depreciation, the greater this year's gross investment is, the greater this year's net investment will be, and equivalently, the greater this year's increase in the capital stock will be. In our example, if gross investment were $700 billion (not $500 billion), then with depreciation still $300 billion, net investment would be $400 billion (not $200 billion), and the increase in the capital stock (*capital accumulation*) would be $400 billion (not $200 billion).

So more gross investment implies more capital accumulation. When I say "investment," I will mean "gross investment," but with depreciation given, more gross investment implies more net investment, or capital accumulation.

Now imagine a simple economy that produces only two goods: corn, the consumption (C) good; and tractors, the investment (I) good. Assume that all available labor, capital, and land will be utilized to produce either corn or tractors. The economic year is beginning. How much labor, capital, and land will be assigned to make tractors, and how much to make corn? Clearly, more labor, capital, and land for tractors means less labor, capital, and land for corn. The tractor production sector—the I sector—can only expand if the corn production sector—the C sector—contracts.

How nice to imagine a world with only corn and tractors. But let's return to the real economy. What belongs in the C sector? The I sector? Obviously, a wheat farm is in the C sector, and a tractor factory is in the I sector. But what about a school? A school should also be in the I sector because it produces human capital. So should the research and development division of every business firm, because the division produces knowledge capital. Capital accumulation increases when a greater share of production occurs in the I sector, and less in the C sector.

Each unit of input—land, labor, or capital—can be assigned to produce goods and services that will be used up—consumed—this year, or to produce goods and services that raise the productive power of workers in the future. The more units of input that are assigned to produce C goods, the fewer that are available to produce I goods.

Imagine a circular pie, representing national output, that is divided into two unequal parts. The large slice is consumption, and the small slice is investment. The only way to increase the investment slice is to reduce the consumption slice. A higher investment rate, or percentage of the pie, today necessitates a lower consumption rate. If more land, labor, and capital are devoted to the production of investment goods, less must be allocated to the production of consumer goods.

So I'm afraid we can't escape a painful truth, no matter what Senator Myopia says. Capital accumulation requires a sacrifice in the present. In order to build machinery (physical capital), improve our skills (human capital), or invent new technology (knowledge capital), time and resources must be diverted away from producing goods and services for current consumption. But does capital accumulation really raise future "productivity" (output per worker)? Let's use some common sense. Why is the productivity of the average American worker today so much higher than the productivity of the average American worker one hundred years ago? Is it because our great grandparents were lazy, and we work hard? Nonsense.

The central reason is that today's American worker has more education and skill (human capital), utilizes more and better machinery and technology (physical capital), and follows a more advanced set of blueprints (knowledge capital).

Compare the primitive farmer, who lacks both a tractor and the skill to operate it, with the modern farmer, who possesses both the tractor (physical capital) and the ability to operate it (human capital). Moreover, the modern farmer utilizes knowledge capital accumulated from past experience, research, and invention, to tell him which farming techniques will be most productive. Is it any wonder that output per worker—productivity—is much higher for the modern farmer?

Countless urban and industrial as well as rural examples make the common-sense point: raising capital per worker generally raises output per worker. Raising capital per worker is therefore the key to raising the standard of living, or consumption per person.

So far I have said nothing about saving. I have explained why capital accumulation through investment is the key to advancing the standard of living, and why raising the investment rate requires reducing the consumption rate. But what about saving? More investment requires more saving, for the simple reason that investment must equal saving. Why?

Saving is defined as income not consumed. Investment is defined as output not consumed. But income must equal output, because for every dollar of output sold, a dollar of income is earned. If output and income are $1,000 billion, and consumption is $900 billion, then income not consumed—saving—is $100 billion; and output not consumed—investment—is also $100 billion.

Keep this simple example in mind. To finance the $100 billion of investment—the purchase of machinery—imagine that business firms issue $100 billion of bonds, and savers purchase the

$100 billion of bonds. In effect, business firms borrow $100 billion from savers (lenders) to invest in $100 billion worth of machinery. The machinery generates a real return—it raises output. Firms use the additional revenue earned on the machinery to pay interest to savers (bondholders). In this example, we can say that the $100 billion of saving is necessary to "finance" the $100 of investment. National income is $1,000 billion. Households choose to consume 90 percent ($900 billion) and save 10 percent ($100 billion). This saving is what makes possible the $100 billion of investment.

So the only way to raise capital accumulation is to raise saving. Raising the national saving rate—the fraction of national income that is saved rather than consumed—is the key to raising the future standard of living.

The saving rate must be raised gradually

But here we are, surrounded by shop windows displaying consumer goods, and I am claiming that raising our saving rate will raise our future standard of living. How can I claim that? If we raise our saving rate, we reduce our consumption rate. But won't this mean less spending at the Mall? And won't the Mall cut its orders from manufacturers of consumer goods? And won't these manufacturers cut production and lay off workers? And won't the result be a recession?

Yes, there would be a recession if we raised the saving rate suddenly and sharply. But there need be no recession if we raise it gradually. Why?

Here's the key point. Today, our economy is a slowly growing economy. If we keep our saving rate the same, output, consumption, and investment all grow at roughly 3 percent per year. All we want to do is to make consumption grow more slowly—say 1 percent per year instead of 3 percent, while we make investment grow more rapidly. If we gradually raise the saving rate, dollar consumption will simply grow more slowly, but it will never actually decline.

When I say we must reduce the consumption *rate* (the fraction of output that we consume) to raise the investment rate, this doesn't mean that dollar consumption must literally decline from one year to the next. So the Mall will never suffer a decline in sales, only a slower growth in sales.

What will happen if the saving rate is raised gradually, or equivalently, if the consumption rate is reduced gradually? As workers voluntarily quit and retire in the consumption goods (C) sector, they will not be replaced. Most new jobs will open up in the investment goods (I) sector. So layoffs will be avoided in the C sector.

Of course, if we were foolish and tried to shift the relative size of the consumption and investment goods sectors too quickly, then we would need to force workers out of the C sector. The result would be layoffs. But by raising the saving rate gradually, we can avoid layoffs. Voluntary quits and retirements will handle the required contraction in the C sector's work force.

But can we be sure that jobs in the I sector will expand enough to prevent a rise in unemployment? As the great economist John Maynard Keynes emphasized in his classic, *The General Theory of Employment, Interest, and Money* (1936), when household demand for consumer goods grows more slowly, this does not guarantee that business demand for investment goods will grow more rapidly. But unless it does, the economy will not generate enough new jobs, and unemployment will rise.

Here is where our central bank, the Federal Reserve ("the Fed") comes in. It is the Fed's job to make sure that the investment goods sector grows more rapidly when the consumer goods sector grows more slowly, so that enough new jobs are created in the economy to prevent unemployment from rising. How can the Fed do this?

Simple. The Fed can reduce interest rates. When interest rates fall, business firms throughout the economy are encouraged to borrow to buy machinery and new technology. They raise their demand for investment goods. The lower the interest rates, the greater the demand for investment goods. In turn, the firms making I goods will need more workers to meet the increased demand. So more new jobs will be created in the I sector.

But how does the Fed lower interest rates? Also simple. The Fed can inject more money into the economy and the banking system. How? By "open market operations," or buying government bonds. The sellers of bonds deposit the money in banks. In response to the infusion of cash reserves, banks try to increase lending. To attract borrowers for their excess funds, banks compete by reducing interest rates. At lower interest rates, business firms find it profitable to buy more investment goods. So the Fed's action results in an increase in investment demand by business firms.

John Maynard Keynes wrote a brilliant book in the 1930s, but it has been misinterpreted. Too many people have become afraid of saving. It is simply not true that an increase in saving must cause a recession. It is only true if the Fed fails to implement routine, appropriate, offsetting monetary policy. Once again, what must the Fed do? When the demand for consumer goods grows more slowly so that few new jobs are created in the C sector, the Fed must make sure that demand for investment goods grows more rapidly so that enough new jobs are created in the I sector. The Fed can easily do this by reducing interest rates, thereby encouraging business firms to borrow to buy more I-sector goods.

But this is all theory. Does it work in practice? Look at other countries. For the past few decades, Japan has had a much higher saving rate than we. So have several European countries. Yet these high-saving countries have not had more recessions, or higher unemployment rates, over these decades. So the theory works in practice. A higher saving rate does not imply a higher unemployment rate.

Let's sum up. If the saving rate is raised gradually, and the Fed earns its pay by proper monetary policy, then our economy can adjust to a higher saving rate without a recession or a rise in unemployment. The higher saving rate means that a larger fraction of our output will be I goods, instead of C goods. Thus, our future output per worker will be higher.

So you thought you were helping the economy by consuming? You asked, "Who will buy goods, if not us? And if we don't buy goods, producers won't make them. And if they don't make them, workers will be laid off. And there will be hard times. So we are patriots when we consume, and traitors when we save."

But now you see your error. You are guilty of the sin of pride. You consumers are not the only buyers of goods in the economy. Business firms buy goods—investment goods. The correct way to look at it is this: the more consumer goods you demand, the more consumer goods producers will make, and the fewer resources—labor, capital, materials, and land—will be available to make investment goods. So you are directly competing with business firms. More consumer goods for you means fewer investment goods for them.

You thought you were heroes, the only buyers in town. Without you, you thought, nobody would buy goods, production would plummet, and down would go the economy. What pride! But you are not the only buyers in town. Business firms are also buyers. And your buying of consumer goods interferes with their buying of investment goods, because the total output of goods that can be produced in a given year is limited.

So don't flatter yourselves. The economy's health does not depend on fast growth in your consumer spending. If you slow the growth of your consumer spending, the Fed will make sure that business firms quicken the growth of their investment spending, and total spending will still grow normally. But now more of the growth in output will be in investment goods, and less in consumer goods.

So, if some economist sets before you a policy that will encourage saving and discourage consumption, do not tremble for the fate of the economy. Such a policy is exactly what is needed to raise the future productive power of the economy. As long as the policy will be phased in gradually, so that it raises the saving rate gradually, do not fear it, but welcome it. Such a policy is economic medicine that is safe and effective.

A common mistake

But I can hear Senator Myopia. At the beginning of this decade, he went around the country blustering, "Who says we can't raise our consumption and investment at the same time? I know how to do it. Let's cut taxes, but don't worry. I won't cut government spending—I don't want to cut your favorite programs. But my tax cut will still work. If I cut your taxes $100, you'll consume $90, and save $10. More saving means more investment, so we'll get more of both—consumption and investment!"

Was he right? Unfortunately, he was not. But where is the mistake? Let's see if we can find it.

First of all, he was right about one thing: if your taxes are cut, you'll consume more. And if you consume more, then the C-goods sector will raise its production. It will draw labor, capital, and land away from the I-goods sector, so production of I goods will be forced down. More corn means fewer tractors. If taxes are cut $100 billion, and households consume $90 billion more, then the I sector will be forced to produce $90 billion less.

If taxes are cut $100 billion, households might raise their saving $10 billion. Doesn't more saving mean more investment? Didn't I say earlier that saving equals investment? So where is the mistake?

True, *national* saving must equal national investment. But national saving is the sum of household, business, and government saving. The tax cut will raise *household* saving. In fact, in our example, households save 10 percent of the tax cut, or $10 billion. The mistake is forgetting about the impact of the tax cut on another component of national saving—government saving.

What is government saving? Saving is always income minus consumption. Therefore, government saving is government net income minus government consumption. Government net income equals tax revenue minus cash "transfer" payments to households or business firms, such as Social Security benefit payments. Government consumption is the purchase of goods or services by government that yield current rather than future bene-

fits to citizens. Actually, most government purchases are investment, rather than consumption, because the goods or services
yield future rather than current benefits. For example, the purchase of labor services for the construction of highways or
schools, or the purchase of military goods such as tanks, yield
benefits primarily in the future. So government saving is determined mainly by government net income—taxes minus transfers.

Now that we have the spotlight on government saving, we can
illuminate Senator Myopia's error. Senator Myopia is holding
government spending constant; he wants you to have all your
favorite programs, including transfers and government consumption. So what happens to government saving when taxes are cut
$100 billion while government spending is held constant?

While households cheer the $100 billion tax cut, the poor
government treasurer is despondent: government net income
falls $100 billion. Since government net income falls $100 billion, and government consumption stays constant, government
saving falls $100 billion.

Since household saving increases $10 billion, but government
saving falls $100 billion, national saving falls $90 billion. So
national investment must also fall $90 billion. And this is exactly
the same answer we obtained before.

Then what is Senator Myopia's mistake? He forgets that household saving is not the same thing as national saving. A $100
billion tax cut may raise household saving $10 billion, but it
reduces national saving $90 billion.

Am I claiming that any tax cut must reduce national saving?
Not at all. Senator Myopia overlooked one little detail. He forgot
to match his tax cut with an equal cut in government transfer
spending. What would have happened if the $100 billion tax cut
were matched by a $100 billion cut in government transfer spend-
ing?

The answer is simple. There would have been no change in
national saving. Taxpayers would have consumed $90 billion
more, but transfer recipients would have consumed $90 billion
less, so there would have been no change in total consumption.

Taxpayers would have saved $10 billion more, but transfer recipients would have saved $10 billion less. Government net income—taxes minus transfers—would have been unchanged, and therefore, government saving would have been unchanged, so there would have been no change in national saving.

Thus, an equal cut in taxes and government transfer spending has no effect on national saving and investment. What hurts national saving and investment, however, is a tax cut that is not matched by an equal cut in government transfer spending. Shame on you, Senator Myopia.

Competition over the future standard of living

But is it really worth raising our saving rate? Is it worth slowing our consumption growth for five or ten years so we can have higher consumption in the future? After all, even at today's saving rate, our future consumption will be higher than our present consumption. Aren't we already saving enough for our future?

If we were alone in the world, the answer might be yes. But we are not alone. There are other countries with higher saving rates, and this implies that eventually—perhaps within a few decades— some nation may attain a higher level of consumption per worker—a higher standard of living.

Do we care about that? Should we care?

First, some facts. Several other nations have been gaining on us since the end of World War II, according to the results of a careful study, shown in Table 2.1.[1]

One reason why these nations are catching up is that they have sustained higher saving rates than we have, as seen in Table 2.2, which shows the ratio of gross saving to gross domestic product from 1960 to 1984 for each nation.[2]

According to one careful comparison of U.S. and Japanese saving rates, conventionally measured saving rates, such as those reported in Table 2.2, do tend to overstate the true gap in properly measured saving. Nevertheless, the authors conclude:

Table 2.1

Per Capita Output Relative to the United States

	1950	1980
United States	100	100
Japan	17	72
Denmark	62	80
France	47	84
West Germany	40	86
Norway	54	90
Sweden	68	85
Switzerland	67	80
Canada	78	93

Table 2.2

Gross National Saving Rates, 1960–1984

Japan	34%
West Germany	25%
France	24%
United States	19%

Despite the fact that our analysis suggests that the disparity in saving rates between the United States and Japan, especially for private as opposed to national saving, is not nearly so large as generally supposed, it is still substantial.[3]

But haven't we been doing better in the 1980s? Hasn't this been the decade of "supply-side economics," when sharp reductions in tax rates were enacted with the promise that they would spur saving? Here's what happened, according to the official data reported in *The Economic Report of the President*, 1988. Gross national saving averaged 16.3 percent of gross national product from 1949 to 1981. (Note that U.S. official data defines the gross saving rate slightly differently from the OECD data reported in

Table 2.2). In the 1970s, it was 16.8 percent. From 1977 to 1980, it was 17.4 percent. But from 1981 to 1987, it was only 14.0 percent.

Net national saving equals gross national saving minus depreciation. It measures whether we are saving enough to actually increase the capital stock. *Net* national saving averaged 8.0 percent of net national product from 1949 to 1981. But from 1982 to 1986, it averaged only 2.7 percent.

But didn't the "supply-side economics" tax cut of 1981 achieve a higher household (personal) saving rate? I'm afraid not. From 1971 to 1980, the personal saving rate averaged 7.9 percent. But from 1981 to 1987, it averaged only 5.5 percent. Even worse, it declined steadily over the decade, dipping to 3.8 percent in 1987.

In an excellent technical analysis of U.S. saving data, in which the authors consider various measures other than the official data, Lawrence Summers of Harvard and Chris Carroll of MIT conclude:

> Even if the fiscal aberration of the Reagan years is corrected, the United States will continue to have a saving problem. Because of the secular downward trend in private saving rates, national saving will be inadequate to finance even the levels of investment that have been observed historically. . . . This leaves a pressing problem for public policy. As long as the U.S. national saving rate lags far behind that of major U.S. competitors, restoring American competitiveness will be difficult.[4] (pp. 633–35)

So whichever measure is used, the conclusion is inescapable: our saving problem, which has been serious for decades, became worse in the 1980s.

I've explained why a nation's future standard of living depends heavily on its saving rate. With our current saving rate, the U.S. absolute standard of living will still rise—slowly—but the U.S. *relative* standard of living will deteriorate in the future. Just as most Americans want to "keep up with the Joneses," most also want to stay ahead of the Japanese. We may wish that Japan would reduce its high saving rate. But if Japan maintains its rate of capital accumulation, threatening to surpass our standard of living perhaps in a few decades, are we willing to fall behind? Even if Japan cannot sustain its rate of capital accumulation, several other nations are actually much closer to overtaking us. It seems likely that some nation will surpass us within a few decades unless we save more.

Some citizens might argue that we should ignore relative comparisons. If Japan, Germany, and France make the sacrifice to achieve a higher standard of living in the future, then that's their decision. We should make our own decision without reference to their behavior. Besides, envy is an unworthy emotion, is it not? Self-confident, ethical individuals should not succumb to envy, or let it govern their behavior, should they?

But concern about relativity may be deeply ingrained. Despite our best efforts, we and our children may be unable to shrug off a deterioration in our relative standard of living. We may suffer "disutility" from a loss of relative status, just as we suffer "disutility" from a loss of absolute income.

The hypothesis that people care about relative position or ranking was given its classic formulation in economics by James Duesenberry in 1949 (*Income, Saving, and the Theory of Consumer Behavior*).

Recently, economist Robert Frank of Cornell University has presented new analysis and evidence supporting the relativity hypothesis in his provocative book, *Choosing the Right Pond: Human Behavior and the Quest for Status*. It is hard to survey the evidence presented by Frank without concluding that, for better or worse, relativity matters a lot to many people.

If we look deeply and honestly within ourselves, we will discover that we Americans count heavily on being second to none. Perhaps we can, and should, be willing to share the lead with several other nations. But falling significantly behind is another matter. Rather than trying to psychologically repress our competitive drive should we not recognize and act on it while we still have time?

It is sometimes asked: Why should we save more so that our children and grandchildren can live still better, when our current saving rate already assures them a better standard of living than ours? If the absolute level of the standard of living were all that mattered, then the question would have merit.

But in a world of international communication and travel, the *relative* standard of living matters. The answer is, we must save more so that our children can maintain the same *relative* standard of living that we enjoy—a standard of living that is second to none. *Relatively*, our children and grandchildren will in fact be worse off than we are if the current trend continues.

Concern about relative standing is grounded in reason as well as emotion. It is difficult to imagine the United States retaining political leadership in world affairs if it surrenders economic leadership. If Western Europe or the Far East surpass the United States economically, our influence abroad will surely diminish. We may find that on crucial foreign policy matters, our leadership is thwarted and we are unable to prevail.

Let us therefore acknowledge that, whether we like it or not, we are engaged in an intergenerational relay race against other nations. Our parents gave us the lead as they passed the baton. Do we care about holding the lead? Are we really content to surrender it, and have our children still waiting for us as they watch their competitors grab the baton and take off? Do we want them to see us as the generation that was given the lead, but was unwilling to make the sacrifice to hold it? Are we willing to subject our children to the foreign policy risks of living in a second-rate economy?

Many Americans do not yet realize what the current trend implies. The American standard of living is currently second to none, and this fact breeds complacency. Most Americans simply do not understand that our relative saving rate today is the key determinant of our relative standard of living tomorrow. And many are unaware that our saving rate is relatively low among economically advanced nations.

Once we Americans resolve to raise our national saving rate, we will discover policies to do it. But these policies will not be seriously considered unless we recognize first the central problem and objective. The problem is that our standard of living and our economic power will not remain second to none indefinitely if our saving rate remains relatively low. Our objective must therefore be to raise our national saving rate.

TECHNICAL APPENDIX
The Economy's Long-run Response
to an Increase in the Saving Rate

Suppose we permanently raise our national saving rate. For example, suppose our saving rate is initially 15 percent (roughly the actual gross saving rate of the U.S. economy), and we raise it to 18 percent permanently. How does the economy respond over the long run?

To answer this question, economists construct a growth model. A growth model can be very complicated, or relatively simple. Let's consider the answer when a relatively simple model is used. The model makes several simplifying assumptions.

First, it assumes that the labor force grows at a steady rate over time. Second, it assumes that production exhibits constant returns to scale. This means that if the amount of labor and capital are each doubled, then output will double. Third, it assumes that labor and capital are each subject to diminishing returns. Meaning that if one factor of production is held fixed, and the other is increased, each successive increase of that factor yields a smaller increase in output. Fourth, initially it assumes there is no technological change.

Now don't make fun of these simplifications. The problem is hard enough even with them. Especially don't laugh at our last simplification—the absence of technological change. I promise we can easily bring it in at the end, and its inclusion will make our analysis more realistic without changing our central conclusion.

Even with these simplifications, it takes a little bit of algebra to work out what happens in the long run when the saving rate is permanently raised. I doubt you're in the mood to do any algebra right now. So the best I can do is tell you the results, try to give you some intuitive understanding, and then send you to some technical treatments if you're really ambitious.[5]

Before we can grasp what happens when the saving rate is raised, we must understand the initial position of the economy. Assume that the saving rate has been 15 percent for a long time. Then according to the model, the economy will have settled into a "steady state." This means that, with no technological change, all "per worker" variables—capital per worker, output per worker, consumption per worker, and saving (investment) per worker—are steady (constant). For example, suppose that output per worker has been holding steady at 100, consumption per worker at 85, and saving (investment) per worker at 15. The model assumes that the labor force is growing at a steady rate—say 1 percent per year. So if capital per worker is staying constant, capital itself must be growing 1 percent per year; and if output per worker is staying constant, output itself must be growing 1 percent per year. So in our initial steady state with a 15 percent saving rate, capital, output, consumption, and saving (investment), are all growing at the same rate as labor—1 percent per year.

Note another point. All per worker variables are constant because we have assumed there is no technological change. Once again, I promise I'll return to technological change shortly. Now, what happens if the saving rate is raised from 15 percent to 18 percent—a 20 percent increase—and then fixed permanently at 18 percent? When we actually adopt policies to raise our saving rate, we must phase them in gradually over several years. But to keep our example simple, let's assume that the saving rate is raised immediately from 15 percent to 18 percent.

At the moment the saving rate is raised, consumption falls, because the consumption rate is being cut from 85 percent to 82 percent. When the consumption rate is cut to 82 percent, output per worker has hardly had time to start rising above its initial value of 100. So consumption per worker will fall from 85 to 82. Please don't be alarmed. We will see shortly that with technological change, and a gradual increase in the saving rate, consumption need not actually decline, contrary to this example. When the saving rate rises from 15 percent to 18 percent, investment per worker rises above its initial value of 15, and this makes capital per worker begin to rise. Why? Because at the 15 percent saving rate, there was just enough investment per worker—15—to make capital grow 1 percent per year, so that capital per worker stayed constant. A saving rate higher than 15 percent means enough investment per worker—more than 15—to make capital grow faster than 1 percent per year, so that capital per worker rises.

But if capital per worker rises, so does output per worker, because machinery raises the output a worker can produce. And this begins to raise consumption per worker, because from now on, consumption will always be 82 percent of output. So after an initial setback, caused when the consumption rate is cut from 85 percent to 82 percent, consumption per worker begins to rise.

It turns out that with the saving rate fixed at 18 percent, the economy will eventually—after many years—converge to a new steady state with higher constant values of capital per worker and output per worker.

Will consumption per worker eventually regain, and surpass, its initial level of 85? There are two opposite forces at work when we raise the saving rate. The lower consumption rate—82 percent instead of 85 percent—tends to reduce consumption, while the rise in output per worker tends to raise it. Which will dominate? Economists have shown, with a little algebra, that as long as the saving rate ends up less than "the capital elasticity,"[6] then consumption per worker will surpass its initial level. In fact, a saving rate equal to the capital elasticity achieves the highest possible consumption per worker in the long run.

According to one study,[7] a plausible estimate of the capital elasticity is roughly 0.37, twice the final gross saving rate of 18

Table 2.3

Response of the Economy to an Increase in Saving Rate

	Output/ worker	Consumption rate	Consumption/ worker
Initial position	100.0	85%	85.0
Year 0	100.0	82%	82.0
Five years	103.7	82%	85.0
Decade	105.8	82%	86.8
Final position	111.2	82%	91.2

percent. Thus, it appears safe to conclude that for increases in the saving rate that our economy might actually undertake, it is virtually certain that in the long run consumption per worker will end up higher than its initial value.

We illustrate with an example based on empirical estimation in the study just cited. Suppose that output per worker ends up at 111.2. Then consumption per worker would end up at 91.2 (82 percent of 111.2). Table 2.3 shows what has happened to consumption per worker.

As the table shows, as soon as the consumption rate is cut to 82 percent, the level of consumption is cut from 85 to 82. But in roughly half a decade, the level of consumption per worker has been restored to its initial level—85—so "the sacrifice time" of the economy is half a decade. Thereafter, consumption per worker exceeds 85. Eventually, output per worker converges to its long-run value of 111.2, and consumption per worker to 91.2 (82 percent of 111.2).

So now we see the choice before us. If we raise the saving rate permanently, we must bear a short-run setback in consumption per worker of roughly half a decade, according to the Lewis-Seidman study. Thereafter, we will achieve a permanently higher standard of living.

In order to make my analysis more realistic, I must now include technological change. To handle it in the simplest possible way, I will assume that it takes a particular form, namely, that it is "labor-augmenting," so that each year it makes each worker more effective or productive. Suppose the rate of technological change is 2 percent per year. Even though the number of workers grows 1 percent per year, "effective labor" grows 3 percent per year because each worker becomes 2 percent more effective each year.

Then it turns out that in the steady state, capital and output will grow 3 percent, not 1 percent, per year, the same as "effective labor." All "per effective labor" variables will be constant in the steady state, and all "per worker" variables will grow 2 percent per year. So in the initial steady state with the 15 percent saving rate, consumption per effective labor is constant, but consumption per worker grows 2 percent per year. The same is true in the final steady state.

The model with technological change fits our economy better. Even with a fixed saving rate, in the steady state all per worker variables grow at the rate of technological change, instead of remaining constant.

But our central conclusion holds. If the saving rate is raised from 15 percent to 18 percent, consumption per worker will grow more slowly in the short run—less than 2 percent. And in the long run the level of consumption per worker will be higher, though its growth rate will again be 2 percent per year. The choice before us will be essentially the same: if we are willing to have slower consumption growth in the short run—for roughly half a decade— then we can enjoy a higher level of consumption per worker in the long run.

Note that in the more realistic model with technological change, the level of consumption per worker may not literally decline as we gradually raise our saving rate from 15 percent to 18 percent. Because consumption per worker is initially growing 2 percent per year, gradually raising the saving rate may cause slower positive growth, not negative growth.

As I emphasized earlier, I am proposing a gradual increase in the saving rate. Our growth model with technological change shows that the result would be slower consumption growth in the short run, but a higher level of consumption per person in the long run.

Notes

1. Robert Summers and Alan Heston, "Improved International Comparisons of Real Product and Its Composition: 1950–1980," *Review of Income and Wealth* 30 (June 1984), 207–262.

2. Organization for Economic Cooperation and Development, *Historical Statistics 1960–1984* (Paris: 1986), table 6.17, p. 70.

3. Michael Boskin and John Roberts, "A Closer Look at Saving Rates in the U.S. and Japan," in John Shoven, ed. *Government Policy Towards Industry in the U.S. and Japan* (New York: Cambridge University Press, 1987), pp. 121–43.

4. Lawrence Summers and Chris Carroll, "Why Is U.S. National Saving So Low?" *The Brookings Papers on Economic Activity* 2 (1987), 607–35.

5. Perhaps the best is by the outstanding innovator in modern growth theory, MIT economist Robert Solow in his *Growth Theory: An Exposition* (New York: Oxford University Press, 1970). An exposition is given in my textbook, *Macroeconomics* (San Diego: Harcourt Brace Jovanovich, 1987).

6. Suppose that with labor held constant, a 1.00 percent increase in capital raises output 0.37 percent. Then "the capital elasticity" is 0.37.

7. Kenneth Lewis and Laurence Seidman, "The Quantitative Consequences of Raising the U.S. Saving Rate," (University of Delaware Department of Economics Working Paper, 1989).

3

MAKE SAVING
TAX DEDUCTIBLE

How can we raise our saving rate? By transforming our tax system. We can state our prescription simply: Make saving tax deductible by converting the income tax to a personal consumption tax.

Many people are gripped by a fear of heresy when they hear this proposal, as if on the sixth day God had said, "Let there be an income tax." True, the income tax has been the centerpiece of the U.S. tax structure for several decades, and the propriety and wisdom of taxing income have come to be taken for granted, a symbol of the American way.

Yet many economists have long advocated taxing consumption, not income. Until recently, however, it has been widely assumed—even by some of these very economists—that taxing each household's consumption might be impractical. And if economists admit that something might be impractical, you can imagine what it's like.

In the last decade, however, a number of practical tax experts—accountants and lawyers—have concluded that a personal (household) consumption tax would be just as impractical and complicated as our income tax, but no worse. Two major studies undertaken by tax specialists—the U.S. Treasury's *Blueprints for Basic Tax Reform* (1977), and the U.K. Institute for Fiscal Studies' *The*

Structure and Reform of Direct Taxation (1978)—even concluded that replacing the income tax with a personal consumption tax would be both feasible and desirable.

The crucial difference between a personal consumption tax and an income tax is simply this: under a consumption tax, saving would be *tax deductible*; every hundred dollars saved would be a hundred dollars that is exempt from tax.

Does a consumption tax favor the affluent?

The most common reaction to the proposal is, "It favors the affluent, who can afford to save." But that reaction is based on a fundamental misunderstanding. Why?

The source of the reaction is the mistaken assumption that the tax rates in the tax tables will be unchanged when saving is made tax deductible. If these tax rates were unchanged, then deductibility would indeed favor the affluent, who can afford to save more.

But who says the tax rates must stay the same? In fact, if the rates were unchanged, then less total revenue would be collected due to the saving deduction, and our budget deficit would get even larger. So when we convert to a consumption tax, and make saving deductible, the rates in the tax table must be raised to keep tax revenue constant. Please note that these rate increases would not raise the dollar tax payment of the average household. They would simply keep the average dollar tax payment the same despite the new saving deduction.

But how should the rate increases be apportioned among income classes? Suppose Congress wants each income class to pay the same revenue it paid under the income tax. Since high income households save most, their tax rate must be raised most. And since low income households save least, their tax rate must be raised least.

So we are advocating conversion of the income tax to an "equally progressive" consumption tax. How do we achieve it? Divide the population into income classes. Calculate the total tax revenue paid by each class under the current income tax. Then set the new tax rates under the consumption tax so that each income class pays roughly the same total tax as before.[1]

Citizens disagree about how the nation's tax burden should be distributed across income classes; they disagree about how "progressive" the tax system should be. The crucial point to grasp is that making saving tax deductible by converting from an income to a personal consumption tax is neutral with respect to distribution. How the rates are set, under either an income or a consumption tax, determines how the burden is distributed across classes. The choice of tax base—income vs. consumption—is completely separate from the choice of distribution—how to set tax rates for each class.

Thus, conversion to a personal consumption tax has been advocated by economists who may disagree about distribution, but agree about the need to raise our national saving rate. For example, two consumption tax advocates are Martin Feldstein, a conservative, and Lester Thurow, a liberal.[2]

So if someone is either for or against conversion because he thinks it favors the affluent, then his reaction is based on a misunderstanding. Congress can make the new consumption tax have more, less, or the same progressivity as the current income tax, simply by adjusting the tax rates in the tax table.

The IRA principle

Making saving tax deductible may sound like a radical departure. It isn't. We've already taken several initial steps in that direction under our income tax.

In the early 1980s, the tax law was amended to allow Individual Retirement Account (IRA) saving to be tax deductible. Unfortunately, the IRA has two key restrictions. First, there is a ceiling on the amount of annual saving that is tax deductible. Second, there is a penalty for withdrawal before retirement. As its name suggests, the purpose of the IRA is to encourage a limited amount of saving for retirement.

Under a personal consumption tax, all saving for any purpose would be tax deductible. There would be no limit on the tax deductible amount. When funds are withdrawn to finance consumption, the consumption would be taxed. But there would be no penalty for withdrawal per se.

The IRA is not the only step we've taken toward a personal consumption tax. Under current tax law, if a person's employer contributes $1,000 to his pension fund, the employee does not pay tax on this $1,000 of income. Because $1,000 of his income has been channeled into saving, it is tax deductible for the employee. Once again, there is an important restriction. The saving must be for retirement.

These restrictions make sense if the aim is to encourage only provision for retirement. But if the aim is to keep our future standard of living second to none, then all saving warrants encouragement. To promote this objective, we must implement the IRA principle more thoroughly by making all saving tax deductible, thereby converting our income tax to a personal consumption tax.

The mechanics of a personal consumption tax

But isn't it impractical to ask everyone to keep receipts of everything they buy? Even an economist can see that. The breakthrough came when some practical person—undoubtedly not an economist—realized that we don't need to add a huge number of purchase receipts to figure out a household's consumption. This ingenious person realized that all we have to do is "follow the cash." We can determine a household's consumption by adding and subtracting only a few items.

The basic insight couldn't be simpler. Almost all consumption is financed by money or checks, which I will call "cash" (perhaps with a short delay made possible by a credit card). We simply follow the cash. A household's cash inflow that is not used for saving or taxes must have been used for consumption. So count the cash inflow. Subtract cash used for saving or tax payments. The remainder must have been used for consumption. So tax it.

For example, suppose a household earns $40,000 in salaries,

$4,000 in interest and dividends, and sells stocks and bonds for $2,000, for a total cash inflow of $46,000. If the household increases its saving account balance by $6,000, buys new stocks and bonds for $2,000, and makes tax payments of $8,000, its total deduction is $16,000. Therefore, its consumption is $30,000 ($46,000 minus $16,000).

I know what you're thinking. What about the treatment of housing and other consumer durables? What about the treatment of gifts and bequests? What about the borderline between consumption and saving? I won't kid you. A consumption tax has some practical problems. They have been examined in detail by experts in the *Blueprints* and elsewhere. Remember, I didn't claim that a consumption tax would be simpler than an income tax, just that it wouldn't be more complicated. I don't advocate a consumption tax for simplicity, but to protect the future standard of living. Here are some possible solutions to these practical problems.[3]

Economists agree that when you purchase a consumer durable, like a car or a house, you are making an investment. Then you consume the services of the durable over many years. So one option is this. If you borrow to finance the durable, the loan can be excluded from cash inflow so only the downpayment is taxed in the year of purchase. But in each subsequent year, you will not be allowed to deduct the loan repayment. Thus, you will be taxed each year on the loan repayment, which is a rough approximation of your consumption that year.

When a donor gives a gift or bequest, he may get pleasure out of it. For that matter, a saver may get pleasure out of saving. But like the saver, the donor is not consuming, he is not drawing resources—land, labor, and capital—away from real investment. His abstaining from consumption helps our future standard of living. If you favor a consumption tax as a weapon in the standard of living race, then you should agree that the gift or bequest should be treated as tax deductible saving to the donor.

What about the donee—the recipient? The gift or bequest is a cash inflow. If he saves it, then he obtains an equal deduction, so the gift or bequest is not taxed. If he ever consumes it, he will be taxed in that year. If he never consumes it, then it will never be taxed. This makes sense, because as long as he abstains from consumption, he helps advance the future standard of living.

Now some consumption tax advocates want the donor to be taxed, some want the donee to be taxed upon receipt, and some want both. They object that gift givers will permanently escape tax, and that this is unfair. They object that donees will escape tax until they actually consume, and that this is unfair. Why is it unfair? Because, they argue, donors and donees may get pleasure or security from gifts and bequests.

But we have a different perspective. Our top priority is the standard of living race. We want to reward our citizens when they help raise the future standard of living. As long as they do not consume, the donor and donee are helping our nation in that race. So they should not be taxed.

Finally, what about the border between consumption and investment? Let me examine one item: education. I know this will sound self-serving, coming from a professor. But the fact is that for at least two hundred years, economists have emphasized that education is an investment in human capital. Like machinery, education raises the productivity of workers. A household's expenditure for education or training should therefore be treated as tax deductible saving under a consumption tax.

Consider what this means. When you set money aside for college tuition while your child is in diapers, it is, of course, tax deductible saving. But even when you withdraw the funds to pay tuition, it remains tax deductible, because an expenditure on education is an investment. So money for college is never taxed.

Despite these possible solutions, there is no denying that the consumption tax has some thorny practical problems. On the other hand, a consumption tax is simpler than an income tax in certain respects.

Consider the little matter of the corporate income tax. The average citizen may have no idea how complicated it is. But one version of a nightmare is to be a new, untrained tax accountant, asked to figure out from scratch what to do about accelerated depreciation, the investment tax credit, corporate mergers and acquisitions, and inventory revaluation. Experts agree that the corporate income tax, with all its complexities, absorbs substantial time from talented accountants, lawyers, and managers, and often results in costly actions. Tax treatment, not genuine productivity, often distorts business decisions.

Under a consumption tax system, there is no justification for a corporate income tax. The reason is simple. Individuals consume, not corporations. So what should we do about the corporate income tax when we convert to a consumption tax? Abolish it. In one stroke, a great source of waste in our economy would be eliminated.

Some consumption tax advocates have been tricked by clever income tax advocates into believing that it is "politically unrealistic" to abolish the corporate income tax. Once they accept this foolish constraint, they are forced to devise another tax on business that is supposedly less harmful to saving and investment than the current tax. The income tax advocates then joyfully recite the complexities of the new business tax. To my consumption tax friends, I say: Don't get trapped. The best solution is to abolish the corporate income tax, period. Abolition can give the business community—not to mention professional economists—something to get excited about. Don't miss an opportunity to do the economically best thing and win some key business support, just because someone tells you that "political realism" requires you to shoot yourself in the foot.

But shouldn't wealthy corporations pay their fair share? Wealthy individuals who consume, yes. Corporations, no. Don't forget what we are trying to do. When a corporation or partnership pays out money to a wealthy individual who consumes, that individual should be taxed at a high rate. But if the business retains the earnings and reinvests them, then no one consumes anything and no one should be taxed. Reinvestment by business helps our nation in the standard of living competition.

But how do we make up for the revenue loss, which would be

about 10 percent of total federal revenue? We do this by setting high enough tax rates on households under the new personal consumption tax. As we explained earlier, rates should be allocated across classes to maintain the same degree of progressivity as the income (personal plus corporate) tax.

The shift in tax revenue from corporations to households may raise private (household plus business) saving.[4] It is likely that the tax shift will cause an increase in corporate retained earnings and a decrease in household disposable (after-tax) income. If household consumption is influenced more by household disposable income than it is by corporate retained earnings—as seems likely—then the tax shift will reduce consumption and raise private saving.

But won't this shift the tax burden from business to people? No. The burden never was borne by business. Every economics textbook underlines this fundamental point: People always bear the whole tax burden. We can pretend this isn't so. But when we tax business, either consumers pay higher prices, employees receive lower compensation, or stock- and bondholders receive less capital income. In all cases, people bear the whole burden.

But won't corporations try to buy cars, vacations, and recreation for employees? Yes, as they do today to avoid income tax for these employees. Just as this is unfair under the income tax system, it would be unfair under a consumption tax. To limit abuse, we need a new IRS regulation that requires the reporting of such expenditures to the IRS, and the imputation of such expenditures to individual employees according to IRS guidelines. In turn, each employee's W-2 form must contain this imputed consumption, which would be included in the employee's taxable consumption.

So here's the political quid pro quo. Business must accept tough IRS regulations and audits to detect any individual consumption occurring through business. In return, business income taxation would be abolished. Most business leaders would find the package attractive.

The horizontal redistribution effect[5]

Conversion to an equally progressive consumption tax will raise national saving. To help make the point as clearly as possible, two affluent persons, each with $100,000 of income, have agreed to be extremists. Person S has agreed to save everything and consume nothing, while person C has agreed to consume everything and save nothing.

Of course, S can only keep this up long enough for readers to grasp the pedagogical point. Rather than ridicule S and C for extremism, be grateful for their voluntary service in the cause of clarity. To compensate them for their service, let's flatter their egos by letting them be the only two people in the affluent $100,000 income class.

Under an income tax of 20 percent, S and C each pay $20,000 in tax, so total affluent tax revenue is $40,000. S saves $80,000 and C, nothing, so total affluent saving is $80,000. C consumes $80,000 and S, nothing, so total affluent consumption is $80,000.

Now Congress makes saving a tax deductible item, and converts the income tax to a consumption tax. What rate must Congress set for the affluent class in order to raise the same total tax revenue, $40,000? Because S and C have graciously agreed to be extremists, the answer is easy. Congressional eyes gaze insidiously on C, who alone will now pay tax. Emaciated S, though weak from lack of nourishment, manages a proud sneer, whispering that he is now exempt from tax. Our Congressmen calculate that if C pays $40,000 in tax, he will consume the remaining $60,000. So, to tax C $40,000 on his $60,000 of consumption, a tax rate of 67 percent is required. Our Congressmen announce that with saving now tax deductible, the tax rate must be raised from 20 percent to 67 percent.

What is the impact of tax conversion? Total tax revenue collected from the affluent remains $40,000. But now, instead of $20,000 coming from each, all $40,000 comes from C. S now, believe it or not, saves all $100,000 of his income, instead of only $80,000, so total affluent saving rises by $20,000 to $100,000.

And since C is forced to cut his consumption due to his higher tax, total affluent consumption falls by $20,000 to $60,000.

What has really happened is this: Tax conversion has caused $20,000 of cash to be redistributed from C to S, because C's cash falls by $20,000 (from $80,000 to $60,000) and S's rises by $20,000 (from $80,000 to $100,000). C would have consumed the $20,000. S saves it. Hence, total affluent consumption falls $20,000, and total saving rises $20,000.

I call this increase in total saving due to the shifting of cash among the affluent *the horizontal redistribution effect*. It is "horizontal" because it is a shift among the affluent, not across different income classes.

Note that the horizontal redistribution effect has nothing to do with the incentive to save. Our two gracious volunteers have agreed to be impervious to incentives. They doggedly stick to their extremist behavior even when saving is made tax deductible. C continues to save nothing, despite the deductibility of saving. And emaciated S would no doubt save more if he could, but he can't, because he's already saving his entire income.

Through the horizontal redistribution effect, making saving tax deductible will raise total saving, even if no one responds to the greater incentive to save. This fundamental point is overlooked in the public debate, even among some sophisticated analysts.

The debate over making saving tax deductible usually runs as follows. Advocates claim that the average individual will raise his propensity to save—the fraction of his after-tax income that he saves—if saving is deductible. Opponents deny it. Both sides assume that total saving will rise only if the typical individual raises his propensity to save.

But our example shows that this is not so. Extremists S and C did not change their propensity to save; S kept it at 100 percent, and C kept it at 0 percent. Each was completely unresponsive to the new incentive to save. But total saving rose through the horizontal redistribution effect. Why? Because deductibility shifted cash away from C, who would have consumed it, to S, who saved it. The horizontal redistribution effect, of course, applies not only to the affluent, but to every income class. Congress can adjust the tax rate of each income class so that the consumption tax raises roughly the same total revenue from that class as did the income tax. But within each class, there will be a horizontal redistribution effect. Above-average savers will enjoy a tax cut, and below-average savers will suffer a tax increase. Cash will shift horizontally from persons with a relatively low propensity to save to persons with a relatively high propensity to save. So total saving will increase.

Although the horizontal redistribution effect applies to all classes, its impact is most important among the affluent. Not surprisingly, there is much more variation in the propensity to save among the affluent than among low income households. Most low income households save very little. But among the affluent, some households save a large fraction of their income, and others dissave—consuming more than their income. For example, in a study done by researchers at the Federal Reserve, roughly 20 percent of affluent households saved two-thirds of their income, another 20 percent saved roughly half, but 20 percent dissaved (consumed more than their income).

A colleague and I used the Federal Reserve data to estimate how much the horizontal redistribution effect would raise total household saving. We estimated an increase of 11 percent.[6]

We can now see clearly whose taxes rise and whose fall by making saving tax deductible and adjusting tax rates to keep the new consumption tax just as progressive as the income tax it replaces. Deductibility does not favor one income class over another. Instead, within each income class, above-average savers enjoy a tax cut, and below-average savers suffer a tax increase; the average saver in the income class pays the same tax.

The incentive to save

Extremist C continued to consume all his after-tax income, despite the deductibility of saving. His consumption fell only because he had less cash. But wouldn't you take advantage of the new deduction by saving a little more? Wouldn't you respond to the new incentive to save? Wouldn't the average person?

How would citizens react to the headline, "Saving Now Tax Deductible"? Word would spread among ordinary taxpayers, not merely shrewd tax planners, that every hundred dollars saved is a hundred dollars not taxed. Many citizens ask: "How can I reduce my taxes?" Now there would be a clear answer: "Save." The subheadline would read: "No Restrictions." The saving can be for any purpose. It can be withdrawn without special penalty. And there is no limit to how much saving is deductible.

Note the difference between open-ended, unrestricted deductibility, and IRAs. With IRAs, a person must worry about whether he is over-saving for retirement. "Suppose I need cash in five years? I'll regret that it's tied up in my IRA." But with unrestricted deductibility, the person must think no further than this year. "If I can get through this year, let me save. I can always withdraw it next year, or in five years, for any purpose, without penalty." Soon, however, a citizen will overcome his enthusiasm with this year's tax saving, and face what happens in the future when he withdraws funds to finance consumption. How will the typical citizen react when he hears the IRS say: "We may not get you now, but we'll get you later"?

Some citizens may succumb in despair. "Why save when it only postpones the ax?" some will ask. But others will react: "Postponement is still worth it. After all, if I'm lucky, the world may end in the meantime." Others, however, will raise this question: "What if I cross the finish line of life, never withdrawing my savings for consumption? What if I leave a large bequest to my heirs at death?"

Good question. Some consumption tax advocates want a bequest at death to be treated as if it were a last dying act of consumption, therefore duly taxable under a consumption tax. These advocates are worried about letting misers sneak across the finish line of life without paying their fair share.

But I'm less worried about our misers than I am about our

nation's future standard of living. The fact is that only actual consumption, not bequests, draws resources away from investment, and reduces our future standard of living. So I side with other consumption tax advocates who say: "If you cross the finish line without consuming, you win; a bequest is not consumption."

While it's only a guess, I suspect that taxing only actual consumption, not bequests, will raise our national saving rate. I have a hunch that the thought of permanently beating the IRS would inspire quite a few citizens to save more. When these citizens hear someone say, "Why save? They'll only get you later when you spend it," these citizens will reply with joy. "They'll never get me, because I'll never spend it; I'll wave it at the IRS from my deathbed, and pass it on to my children and grandchildren."

The great postponer

When taxes are compared, attention focuses on incentives. But there is another crucial aspect of taxes that is usually overlooked: which tax most postpones collection over an individual's "life cycle"?

Perhaps the most important property of the consumption tax is this: it is *"the great postponer."* For this reason, as much as any other, a consumption tax should result in a greater accumulation of capital in the economy than an income tax.

Imagine that each individual is a "life cycler." A life cycler plans ahead. He recognizes that someday he will retire, and upon retirement, alas, his income will fall further than his desired consumption. While he works, he must save, so that he can dissave in retirement to finance his consumption. Of course, not everyone is a life cycler, but enough people plan ahead, however imperfectly, to make the life cycler worth studying.

A life cycler's consumption is less than his income during most of his work life, and greater than his income during retirement. Thus, when the income tax is converted to a consumption tax, the young person just beginning his life cycle will enjoy a tax cut during his work life, and will incur a tax increase in retirement.

Conversion causes postponement of some of his lifetime tax.

But this means that conversion to a consumption tax increases the ability of workers to save and accumulate wealth. Tax postponement therefore results in greater accumulation of wealth by the typical life cycler, and hence, a greater capital stock for the economy.

Thus, a consumption tax should achieve a higher capital stock than an income tax for three reasons: the horizontal redistribution effect, the incentive effect, and the postponement effect.[7]

Is a consumption tax equivalent to a labor income tax?

Instead of a saving deduction, why not enact a capital income exemption? Under this alternative tax reform, you wouldn't get a deduction when you save. But when you earn interest, dividends, or capital gains, your capital income would be exempt from tax. Like a saving deduction, a capital income exemption gives an incentive to save.

A saving deduction converts the income tax into a consumption tax. A capital income exemption converts the income tax into a labor income tax. Both conversions give the incentive to save. For this reason, some analysts have claimed that a consumption tax is really equivalent to a labor income tax.

But it isn't. And it is crucial to understand why.

While the consumption tax is "the great postponer," the labor income tax is "the great upfronter." Under a labor income tax, the government raises all tax revenue from workers, and none from retirees. So a life cycler pays all his tax "up front"—during the work stage of life. Compared to a consumption tax, a labor income tax imposes a greater tax burden on the worker, thereby reducing his ability to save. Hence, a labor income tax would achieve a smaller capital stock than a consumption tax.

In fact, the labor income tax is more of an upfronter than the regular income tax, which at least postpones some tax to retirement. So it is even possible that, despite its incentive to save, a labor income tax would achieve a lower capital stock than a regular income tax. By contrast, a consumption tax gives the incentive to save, and is also a greater postponer than an income tax, so it will clearly achieve a higher capital stock for the economy.

The labor income tax gives the worker an incentive to save, but reduces his ability to do so. The consumption tax gives the worker an incentive to save, and improves his ability to do so. Since the consumption tax should result in a significantly larger capital stock than the labor income tax, it makes no sense to call them equivalent.

The two taxes also differ fundamentally with respect to fairness. The best way to communicate this difference is to shine the spotlight on a notorious character: the lazy heir. For some, the only worth of this brazen individual is his pedagogical value. For others, he is a source of secret admiration. At any rate, who is he? The lazy heir inherits a large fortune, uses it to finance a high level of consumption, never works a day in his life, and dies leaving nothing to his own children, because, he says, he doesn't wish to spoil them.

Now, what tax would the lazy heir owe under a labor income tax? Zero. At the annual April 15 news conference at his plush estate, the lazy heir holds up his tax return—an empty sheet of paper. With servants surrounding him, he complains that it is most fortunate that he owes no tax, not having worked, because he needs every bit of his fortune to maintain his mansion. Needless to say, he is a favorite on the evening news.

Under a consumption tax, however, the plight of our lazy heir would be severe. His high consumption would incur a high tax. As he sold the stocks and bonds he inherited, his cash inflow would record the sale of assets. Since there is no corresponding deduction, his taxable consumption would match his asset sales.

In fact, a consumption tax would tax the lazy heir more heavily than an income tax. Under an income tax, he would be taxed on capital income. But under a consumption tax, he would be taxed on the wealth he "decumulated" each year. Suppose the lazy heir were, for spite, to convert his fortune to cash, and place it under his luxurious pillow so that it earned no income. He would owe no income tax. But he would still owe substantial consumption tax.

Thus, with respect to fairness, a consumption tax is surely not equivalent to a labor income tax. Under a consumption tax, anyone enjoying high consumption would owe a high tax. The same would not be true with a labor income tax, as the case of the lazy heir dramatically illustrates.

How to gradually phase in a personal consumption tax

Conversion to a consumption tax must be phased in gradually for two distinct reasons: to assure a smooth macroeconomic transition, and to avoid double taxation. Let's consider each in turn.

First, macroeconomics. Recall what we are trying to do. We want to gradually raise the percentage of our national economic pie that goes to investment. This requires that we gradually reduce the percentage that goes to consumption. But our pie per person grows in a typical year. So it is possible to gradually reduce the percentage that goes to consumption without ever reducing the absolute size of the consumption slice per person. This should be our aim: to gradually reduce the percentage without ever reducing the absolute amount per person.

We want to slow the growth of consumer goods, so that workers who quit or retire in the consumer goods sector are not replaced, and most new jobs open up in the rapidly growing investment goods sector. But we do not want to make the output of consumer goods literally decline, because this would result in involuntary layoffs and a transitional recession. No one knows how much our population would cut its consumption demand if the entire population were converted to the consumption tax in a single year. It would therefore be completely irresponsible to convert the whole population at one time.

Now let's consider the double taxation problem. Under an income tax, a person pays tax on the income he saves, but no tax on his retirement consumption. Under a consumption tax, a person pays no tax on the income he saves, but pays tax on his retirement consumption. Now consider the "lucky" person who gets caught in the transition. He has paid tax on the income he saved. And he will also pay tax on his retirement consumption. He has a complaint: "I've been double taxed."

Here's one way to handle both problems. First, for macroeconomic smoothness, the population would be phased in in stages. Perhaps the simplest criterion would be the age of the head of the household. For example, in year one, all households with the "head" (the older member) age 25 or under would be permanently converted to the consumption tax. In year two, all households with the head between 27 and 32; in year three, all households with the head between 34 and 39; and so on. In roughly a decade, the whole population would be under the consumption tax.

This age-based phase-in has several advantages. With age, there is relatively little game playing. You know which tax you are under, and there is little you can do about it (except to change your marital status). It's simple. You never have to compute both an income tax and a consumption tax; you are either under one tax, or the other, and you know which when the year starts. Finally, once you convert, you convert for life.

Second, to avoid double taxation, each household would list the assets it holds on the first day of the year it enters the consumption tax system. When the household sells an asset, it would be permitted a deduction equal to the "basis" of the asset.

What would determine an asset's basis? Consider assets that have never been taxed—qualified pensions and tax-sheltered savings accounts. Under the income tax, they would be fully taxed upon withdrawal. Thus, they would have a zero basis, and would be fully taxed upon withdrawal under the consumption tax.

Next, consider stocks and bonds. Under the income tax, any capital gain—revenue minus cost—would be subject to tax. Thus, stocks and bonds would have a basis equal to the purchase cost, so that the excess of revenue over cost would be fully taxed under the consumption tax. For example, suppose the stock market rose in response to the abolition of the corporate income tax. Stock-holders would be fully taxed on the rise if and when they sold stocks to finance consumption.

Note how the double taxation protection helps handle the macroeconomic problem. Suppose preexisting assets were not protected. Then imagine a middle-age person who knows he will convert to the consumption tax in several years. He has a strong incentive to consume his preexisting assets prior to conversion in order to avoid double taxation. But the basis deduction eliminates this incentive. Thus, the double taxation protection enables the gradual age-based phase-in that is essential for a safe, smooth, macroeconomic transition.[8]

Let's use this powerful tool

We are engaged in an international competition over the future standard of living. And we need to do better. If the current trend continues, within a few decades we may no longer be second to none. Perhaps the single most important reason why is that our saving rate lags behind that of several other nations. Our tax system is one important tool for raising our saving rate and protecting our future relative standard of living. So let's unleash this powerful tool. The time has come to make saving tax deductible by converting our income tax to a personal consumption tax.

Notes

1. Of course, a given income class may not pay the same revenue as before because its response to the saving deduction differs from the response predicted by the technicians who will advise Congress concerning tax rates. The actual response can be taken into account the next time rates are adjusted. Note that tax revenue cannot be predicted accurately under the income tax either.

2. Martin Feldstein, "Taxing Consumption," *The New Republic*, 28 February 1976, pp. 14–17; and Lester Thurow, *The Zero-Sum Solution* (New York: Simon and Schuster, 1985), pp. 237–38.

3. I am indebted to these authors for their analysis of practical aspects of a personal consumption tax: Henry Aaron and Harvey Galper, *Assessing Tax Reform* (Washington, D.C.: Brookings Institution, 1985); David Bradford,

Untangling the Income Tax (Cambridge: Harvard University Press, 1986); William Andrews, "A Consumption-Type or Cash Flow Personal Income Tax," *Harvard Law Review* 87 (April 1974), 1113–88; and Michael Graetz, "Expenditure Tax Design," in Joseph Pechman, ed. *What Should Be Taxed: Income or Expenditure?* (Washington, D.C.: Brookings Institution, 1980), pp. 161–295.

4. Gross business saving is roughly 80 percent, and personal (household) saving is 20 percent, of gross private saving.

5. This section is based on Laurence Seidman, "The Personal Consumption Tax and Social Welfare," *Challenge* 23 (September 1980), 10–16.

6. Stephen Maurer and Laurence Seidman, "The Consumption Tax, Horizontal Redistribution, and Aggregate Saving," *Mathematical Modelling: An International Journal* 5:4 (1984), 205–222. Maurer and I analyze the long-run impact of the horizontal redistribution effect in "Taxes and Capital Intensity in a Two-Class Disposable Income Growth Model," *Journal of Public Economics* 19 (November 1982), 243–59.

7. The postponement effect is demonstrated in Lawrence Summers, "Capital Taxation and Accumulation in a Life Cycle Growth Model," *American Economic Review* 71 (September 1981), 533–44; and in Laurence Seidman, "Taxes in a Life Cycle Growth Model With Bequests and Inheritances," *American Economic Review* 73 (June 1983), 437–41.

8. Further analysis is given in Laurence Seidman, "Conversion to a Consumption Tax: The Transition in a Life Cycle Growth Model," *Journal of Political Economy* 92 (April 1984), 247–67.

4

BALANCE THE BUDGET
SAFELY WITH NUBAR

Should the government try to balance its budget every year? Most citizens say yes, but most economists say no. Most citizens think the issue is simple; most economists think it's complicated. I know. Now you're sure it's simple. But hear me out.

Economists believe that it would be bad to balance the budget every year. They disagree over whether it is even good to balance the budget, on average, over a decade. And they disagree about whether any kind of balanced budget rule should be enacted, either as a statute or a constitutional amendment.

I will try to explain why economists find the issue complicated. But I have no intention of leaving you in despair. Once I have led you into the wilderness of complexity and we have wandered together for a few minutes, I will then show you a way out. And this way out will be a statute called **NUBAR**—my own acronym— which stands for "**n**ormal **u**nemployment **ba**lanced budget rule," and which reads as follows: "Congress shall enact a budget for the coming fiscal year that is estimated to be balanced *on the assumption that the unemployment rate will be normal (the average of the preceding decade)*."

You'll admit that NUBAR is not very complicated. But you're probably thinking, why not make it even simpler by dropping that clause about the normal unemployment rate. In fact, that's exactly what our current balanced budget statute, the famous Gramm-Rudman-Hollings (GRH), does. It's even simpler than NUBAR, because it says nothing about the normal unemployment rate.

But simplicity isn't everything. That little clause makes all the difference. Its omission means that Gramm-Rudman-Hollings would destabilize the economy.

I have no choice but to be harsh about this little flaw in the current design of GRH. After all, destabilizing the economy is not exactly a trivial defect. But I don't want to appear ungrateful to Gramm-Rudman-Hollings. On the contrary, NUBAR copies two breakthrough features of GRH, and authors of GRH deserve credit for these important innovations.

First, like GRH, NUBAR places fiscal policy under a statutory rule, rather than leaving it to the discretion of Congress and the president. And second, NUBAR utilizes the infamous enforcement mechanism of Gramm-Rudman-Hollings: the automatic, uniform, across-the-board cut of spending to assure compliance. So NUBAR's debt to GRH is deep.

Let's come right out and admit it. NUBAR isn't a perfect rule. In fact, later I will even mention a better, though more complicated, rule. And I'll acknowledge merit in the points made by several sophisticated critics of NUBAR.

But I approach the balanced budget issue inspired by the wise old aphorism: "The best is the enemy of the good." There's no point pretending. A NUBAR statute falls short of the best in several respects, as we shall see. Yet I will argue that, despite its faults, NUBAR is the statute we should urge Congress to enact.

So the recommendation of this chapter is simple: Insert the following bold-faced clause into Gramm-Rudman-Hollings: "*on the assumption that the unemployment rate will be normal (the average of the preceding decade)*."

A balanced budget rule and the national saving rate

Why do we want a balanced budget rule? Because shifting our

average budget from deficit to balance will raise national saving. Why? Prepare for a few paragraphs of exciting, inescapable accounting.

National saving is the sum of private saving plus government saving. But what is government saving? As we explained in chapter 2, saving is defined as net income minus consumption, so government saving equals government net income (taxes minus transfers such as Social Security benefit payments) minus government consumption purchases of goods and services. Imagine you're the government treasurer. If taxes increase $100 billion, or transfers are cut $100 billion, or government consumption purchases are cut $100 billion, then "your" (government) saving increases $100 billion.

An effective balanced budget statute would raise government saving. Why? In order to move from a deficit to a balanced budget, taxes must be raised or spending cut. But raising taxes, cutting transfer spending, or cutting government consumption purchases, would each raise government saving. Only cutting government investment purchases of goods and services (such as expenditures on highway construction) would have no effect on government saving. As long as the budget is not balanced entirely by cutting government investment spending, the statute will raise government saving.

In the 1980s, the government deficit has averaged roughly 4 percent of gross national product (GNP). Under a balanced budget rule, this 4 percent gap would be eliminated. If less than half of this 4 percent gap is closed by a cut in government investment spending, then government saving would rise by more than 2 percent of GNP due to the balanced budget statute.

I must confess that the increase in *national* saving will be a little smaller. Suppose taxes rise $100 billion, raising government saving $100 billion. Then private saving may fall $5 billion (our personal saving rate is 5 percent), so that national saving will rise $95 billion, instead of $100 billion. But this slight offset in private saving does not alter the main point. A balanced budget statute would raise government saving, and hence, national saving.

An always-balanced budget rule is destabilizing

To many citizens, the remedy for government deficits seems simple: require a balanced budget every year. According to this view, the planned budget should always aim at balance, based on the best available forecast. Once the fiscal year has begun, if a deficit begins to emerge, a prompt cut in spending or increase in taxes to restore balance should be required. I'll call this an "always-balanced budget rule." Another name might be, "the no ifs, ands, or buts balanced budget rule," or "the no excuses balanced budget rule." The rule is so simple. It's a shame it suffers from a fatal defect: it would destabilize the economy. Why?

Suppose the economy is operating at a normal level of output when the budget for next year is planned. Technicians advise Congress on where to set tax and spending rates so that if the economy remains normal, the budget will be balanced.

How do the technicians arrive at their conclusion? They estimate how much tax revenue will be raised—given the statutory tax rates—if the economy is normal and national income is normal; they then compare this revenue to estimated expenditure. Make note of this: if national income turns out to be below normal, then tax revenue will be lower than the technicians' estimate.

As the fiscal year begins, suppose the economy falls into recession. National income falls below normal and, automatically, tax revenue falls below the level that planners expected. Hence, the budget moves into deficit.

If you are inclined to blame Congress for everything, please note that this particular deficit is not the fault of Congress. The source of this deficit is the unexpected recession. But this is a "no excuses" balanced budget rule. Even though Congress did not cause the deficit, it must act promptly to eliminate it. Under the always-balanced rule, Congress must promptly cut spending or raise tax rates to eliminate the deficit brought on by recession.

What happens to the economy, already in recession, when Congress cuts spending or raises taxes? Suppose Congress cuts government purchases. For example, it cuts the purchase of planes for the military, and computers for government offices. Then the producers of planes and computers suffer a fall in orders, and hence, cut production. Their employees earn less income, and in turn, cut their consumer spending. The recession deepens.

Or suppose Congress cuts cash transfers. For example, it cuts spending on welfare, food stamps, and college financial aid. Then the recipients of these transfers have less to spend, and producers observe a decline in demand. They cut production. Their employees earn less income, and in turn cut their consumer spending. Once again, the recession deepens.

Finally, suppose Congress raises tax rates. Taxpayers have less after-tax income, cut their spending, and the result is the same: an intensification of the recession. Thus, no matter how Congress tries to eliminate the recession-induced deficit, it makes the recession worse.

For decades, economics textbooks have emphasized that an always-balanced budget rule is destabilizing. Unfortunately, some important public officials have yet to grasp the point. In 1985, the Senate Judiciary Committee reported an always-balanced budget constitutional amendment. It read as follows: "Section 1. Outlays of the United States for any fiscal year shall not exceed receipts to the United States for that year. . . ."

Undoubtedly, the drafters sought simplicity, and an always-balanced budget rule is beautifully simple. However, such a rule destabilizes the economy. It requires fiscal action that makes a recession worse. There's no point denying this. A rule that makes Congress take action causing a recession to worsen is not a very good rule.

A forecasted balanced budget rule is also destabilizing

What about a rule that requires a *planned* balanced budget, but does not require mid-year fiscal action if a deficit emerges due to recession? At first glance, it might appear that a planned balanced budget rule avoids the destabilization problem. Apparently, the designers of the Gramm-Rudman-Hollings statute thought so, because GRH focuses on the planned budget. And the designers of the 1984 Senate Judiciary balanced budget constitutional amendment thought so, because that amendment also focuses on the planned budget. That amendment begins as follows: "Section 1. Prior to each fiscal year, the Congress shall adopt a statement of receipts and outlays for that year in which total outlays are not greater than total receipts."

But is it true that focusing on the planned budget avoids destabilization? Unfortunately, the answer is no. If the planned budget must be estimated to be balanced according to a forecast of next year's economy, then the planned balanced budget rule will also be destabilizing. Why?

Suppose a normal economy is initially forecast for the coming fiscal year. Based on this forecast, technicians set tax and expenditure rates so that, by their estimation, the budget will be balanced. But just prior to the budget's final passage, the forecast changes to recession. What happens?

With the initial tax and expenditure rates, technicians now estimate that the budget will be in deficit, because tax revenues are lower in a recession. To make the planned budget yield an estimate of balance, either expenditure rates must be cut, or tax rates increased.

But if Congress so shifts the planned budget, it will make the recession worse. A cut in expenditure rates will reduce demand in the economy, as will an increase in tax rates. So if the forecast is accurate and the recession materializes, the shift in the planned budget will only intensify it.

Unlike the always-balanced budget, no new fiscal action is required when the recession emerges. But this is only because the destabilizing action has been taken *in advance*, when the planned budget was finalized. When a recession is suddenly forecast, the planned budget is shifted to try to maintain balance despite the forecasted recession, and this shift intensifies the recession if it occurs.

Thus, the fundamental source of destabilization is the attempt to balance the budget regardless of the state of the economy. Designers of balanced budget rules must grasp this crucial point: It is bad to try to balance the budget every year. The designers of Gramm-Rudman-Hollings recognized that applying the forecast-based rule in a recession would be destabilizing. They therefore included an ad hoc suspension of the rule in recession. But there are two serious shortcomings with this attempted solution.

First, once the suspension is triggered, Congress is free to enact any budget it wants. So Congress will probably take advantage of suspension years to make up for the restraint of binding years. It seems likely that especially large planned deficits will be enacted in suspension years. So it is possible that, with the suspension, the statute will not succeed in reducing the average deficit over a decade. Large suspension-year deficits may offset binding-year balanced budgets. If so, the statute won't raise the national saving rate over the decade.

Second, by the same logic, there should be a suspension for booms. Suppose that just prior to the budget's final passage, the forecast changes to a boom. With the initial tax and expenditure rates, technicians now estimate that the budget will be in surplus because, in a boom, tax revenues will be higher. To make the planned budget yield an estimate of balance, either expenditure rates must be raised, or tax rates cut.

But if Congress so shifts the planned budget, it will intensify the inflationary boom. A rise in expenditure rates or a cut in tax rates will raise demand in the economy. So if the forecast is accurate, and the boom materializes, the shift in the planned budget will intensify inflation.

Gramm-Rudman-Hollings does not have a boom suspension. After all, to have both a boom suspension and a recession suspension would mean that the statute would be suspended most of the time. And that would be embarrassing, because there is obviously something wrong with a statute that needs to be suspended most of the time. What must be grasped is that an automatic modification of the target—a balanced budget—is needed whenever an abnormal economy is forecast. A sound rule would require planners to aim for a balanced budget in a normal economy, but not in an abnormal economy. But rule suspensions are no answer. There must be a constraint on the planned budget in the abnormal years—a constraint that prevents destabilizing behavior, but at the same time causes the budget to be balanced, on average, over a decade.

Can this be done? Fortunately, the answer is yes.

A solution: NUBAR

As stated above, the following simple balanced budget rule would avoid destabilization: "Congress shall enact a budget for the coming fiscal year that is estimated to be balanced *on the assumption that the unemployment rate will be normal (the average of the preceding decade).*"

I call this rule NUBAR (normal unemployment balanced budget rule). Why does NUBAR avoid destabilization? Because a change in the forecast does not result in a shift in the planned budget.

Return to my first example. Recall that just prior to final enactment of the budget, next year's forecast changed to recession. If the forecasted budget must be estimated to be balanced, then either expenditure rates must be cut or tax rates raised. But with NUBAR, the change in the forecast is irrelevant. Why?

Under NUBAR, expenditure and tax rates are in compliance as long as the budget would be balanced in a normal economy. Hence, NUBAR would not permit, much less require, a destabilizing shift in the planned budget in response to a change in the forecast.

In effect, then, NUBAR attempts to balance the budget only in a normal economy. If the economy is in recession, NUBAR implicitly plans a deficit. If the economy is in a boom, NUBAR implicitly plans a surplus. Over a decade, the average position of the budget will be close to balanced. Thus, NUBAR does not attempt to balance the budget each and every year, regardless of the state of economy. Instead, it settles for the goal of achieving an average position of the budget, over a decade, that is close to balanced.

NUBAR is not a novel proposal. For many years, economists have recommended that Congress try to balance "the full employment budget," not the actual budget. The "full employment budget" is the budget that would occur if the economy were at its maximum feasible output. Like NUBAR, this rule makes the planned budget independent of any change in the forecast. It therefore avoids destabilization. Thus, the basic strategy of NUBAR has long been advocated by economists. There are, however, two differences between NUBAR and the "full employment balanced budget rule." First, NUBAR avoids a debate about what is "full employment." Instead, NUBAR uses the normal unemployment rate as its benchmark. The normal unemployment rate is defined as the average of the preceding decade. "Normal" is not necessarily "optimal" or "full."

Second, NUBAR will achieve an average budget deficit, over a decade, that is close to zero, because it is based on a realistic unemployment rate—the actual average of the preceding decade. A full employment budget rule will achieve an average budget deficit, over a decade, that is much greater than zero. The reason is that, in practice, Congress will undoubtedly define "full employment" more ambitiously than normal employment.

For example, under NUBAR, if the average unemployment over the preceding decade has been 7 percent, then NUBAR will require a planned budget that is balanced on the assumption that the economy's unemployment rate will be 7 percent. We do not claim 7 percent is "optimal" or "full"; it is simply realistic, "normal." A full employment balanced budget rule might require a planned budget that is balanced on the assumption that the economy's unemployment rate will be, say, 5 percent, or even 4 percent. But when the economy's unemployment rate turns out, on average, to be closer to 7 percent, this planned budget will result in a deficit.

Thus, in practice, NUBAR should achieve tighter budgets than a "full employment" balanced budget rule. Government saving and hence, national saving, will therefore be higher under NU-BAR. While both rules would avoid destabilization, NUBAR is preferable with respect to our goal of raising the national saving rate.

The Phase-In

Any balanced budget rule should be phased in over several years. NUBAR is just as relevant to the transitional deficit targets. During the transitional phase, the rule should read: "Congress shall enact a budget for the upcoming fiscal year that is estimated to achieve the deficit target on the assumption that the unemployment rate will be normal (the average of the preceding decade)."

If an actual forecast, rather than the normal unemployment rate, is used during the transition, destabilization will occur. For example, suppose the transitional deficit target is $100 billion. If an initial unemployment forecast of 7 percent shifts, just prior to budget enactment, to 9 percent, then a forecasted budget rule requires a cut in spending rates or an increase in tax rates to achieve a planned deficit of $100 billion. But this shift in the planned budget would reduce total demand in the economy, and intensify the recession. Thus, NUBAR is as urgently needed in the transition phase as after it.

The best is the enemy of the good

NUBAR is a good rule, although it is not "the best." Yet refusing to accept anything less than the ideal rule may condemn us to the status quo. This practical warning should be heeded as we discuss the following criticisms of NUBAR.

"NUBAR doesn't stabilize the economy." This accusation is correct. NUBAR makes fiscal policy neutral. In sharp contrast to the always-balanced rule and the forecasted rule (like Gramm-Rudman-Hollings and the 1984 constitutional amendment), NU-

BAR would avoid destabilizing the economy. But it is true that NUBAR does not permit a shift in the budget that would try to combat a recession or boom.

A rule could be designed that would require shifts in the budget to stabilize the economy. In a recession, the rule would require a larger planned deficit than NUBAR, so that a spending increase or tax cut would add stimulus. In a boom, the rule would require a larger planned surplus than NUBAR, so that a spending cut or tax increase would reduce stimulus.[1]

Such a rule would probably be better than NUBAR. But it would also be more complex, and more difficult for legislators and citizens to understand. Here's what such a statute would look like:

> Congress shall enact a budget for the coming fiscal year that is estimated to achieve the "targeted" ratio of deficit to gross national product on the assumption that the unemployment rate will be normal.
>
> The "targeted" ratio of deficit to gross national product shall depend on the current unemployment rate:
>
> 1. If the current unemployment rate equals the normal unemployment rate, then the targeted ratio shall be 0 percent.
>
> 2. If the current unemployment rate is greater than the normal rate, then the targeted ratio shall be raised 0.5 percent for each 1 percent by which the current rate exceeds the normal rate.
>
> 3. If the current unemployment rate is less than the normal rate, then the targeted ratio shall be reduced by 0.5 percent for each 1 percent by which the normal rate exceeds the current rate.

If economists press for this rule, it is likely that Congress will reject it as too complex and unintelligible, and we will continue to have no rule, or a destabilizing rule like the current Gramm-Rudman-Hollings. A better strategy is to urge Congress to adopt NUBAR. Once a NUBAR statute is enacted, we can then consider whether NUBAR should in turn be replaced by the more complex stabilizing rule.

But if NUBAR is neutral, who will stabilize the economy? The answer, we will argue in chapter 7, is our central bank, the Federal Reserve. The Federal Reserve is the institution best suited to bear the responsibility for stabilizing the economy by the proper conduct of monetary policy.

In contrast to Congress, which has hundreds of tasks, the Fed has only a few. It meets monthly, relatively insulated from political pressure, to adjust monetary policy with the aim of stabilizing the economy. It has a talented staff of well-trained economists who focus on this task. If the economy is in recession, the Fed raises the money supply, reducing interest rates to provide stimulus. If the economy is in a boom, the Fed contracts the money supply, raising interest rates to provide restraint.

NUBAR would make the Fed's task easier. The Fed cannot set the proper monetary policy unless fiscal policy is predictable. With no rule governing fiscal policy, the Fed must guess what Congress will do. This is no easy task. But if Congress is constrained by NUBAR, the Fed can plan more effectively.

The burden of stabilizing the economy should not be assigned to Congress. Instead, the aim should be to constrain Congress so that, on average, the budget is close to balance, and destabilizing budget shifts are avoided. Given this neutral, predictable fiscal policy, it should then be the Fed's job to stabilize the economy.

"A balanced budget rule ignores government investment." This accusation has merit. Government saving is defined as government net income (taxes minus transfers) minus government purchases for consumption. But the government surplus (which we call 'deficit' when it is negative) is defined as government net income (taxes minus transfers) minus *all* government purchases—for investment as well as consumption.

If our aim is to raise national saving, then the ideal rule would be a target for government saving, not the government surplus or deficit. Government saving is not increased if government purchases for investment—highways, bridges, dams, and so forth—are cut, even though this helps to reduce the government deficit and balance the budget.

But there is a practical problem with a government saving rule.

Government investment must be distinguished from government consumption. This is no easy task in many cases. Legislators would have a strong incentive to define any government purchase as investment, so that it can be raised despite the government saving target.

A balanced budget rule puts pressure on taxes, transfers, and government purchases for consumption; this pressure raises government saving and hence, national saving. But it also puts pressure on government purchases for investment, and this pressure has no effect on government saving.

Is the pressure on government investment desirable? This is a complex issue. If the return on government real investment exceeds the return on private investment, then the pressure would be undesirable. But if government investment yields a lower return than private investment, then the pressure is desirable, because it would be better if a greater fraction of national saving were directed toward the private sector.

But it is difficult to measure the return on government investment. For example, consider a highway. A private firm would try to maximize revenue by its toll structure. But government often does not try to maximize toll revenue. Thus, the return on this government investment, measured by toll revenue, is less than the return a private firm would achieve. In this case, the measured return understates the social return on the investment.

On the other hand, notorious "pork barrel" projects often have a low return. Private firms would never undertake them. But they are politically profitable to individual legislators. It would clearly be desirable to have the promoters of these projects feel pressure from a balanced budget rule.

So it is unclear whether a balanced budget rule applies the right degree of pressure to government investment. But the pressure it applies to taxes, transfers, and government consumption spending all tend to raise the national saving rate. The best should not be an excuse to prevent the good.

"The government deficit is measured incorrectly." The charge is correct. Economists like Robert Eisner of Northwestern Uni-

versity have explained some of the shortcomings of conventional measurement. But we need not go into details, because the argument does not undermine the case for NUBAR. Why?

Suppose a conventionally measured deficit of $50 billion implies a properly measured deficit of $0. If NUBAR uses conventional measurement, it would require a shift in the budget to achieve a conventionally measured planned budget of $0, which might imply a properly measured surplus of $50 billion. Is this undesirable?

If the goal were to balance the correctly measured budget, aiming at conventionally measured balance would obviously be undesirable. But if the goal is to raise the national saving rate above its current level, then aiming at conventionally measured balance is still desirable. As long as reducing the conventional deficit generally corresponds to raising national saving, then the rule is desirable, despite measurement error.

"Raising government saving does not always raise national saving." This assertion is theoretically correct, because it is possible for the increase in government saving to induce an offsetting reduction in private saving.

For example, suppose there were no Social Security system, and that individuals saved privately for retirement. Now suppose Social Security is enacted, but unlike our actual system, it is to be financed like a properly run private pension. Upon introduction, workers are taxed, but no benefits are paid, so that a genuine fund accumulates. Then as each worker retires, he draws down the fund he has built by tax contributions (plus interest).

In the first years after enactment, the Social Security tax raises revenue, but there is no government spending, so government saving increases, and the government deficit—including the Social Security account—is reduced. But there may be no increase in national saving. Why? Because individuals may cut their private saving by an amount equal to the government saving done on their behalf. For example, for each $100 of additional payroll tax, a worker may cut his private saving $100, because he views his payroll tax as a form of saving.

Thus, some forms of government saving may trigger a corresponding cut in private saving. Economist Laurence Kotlikoff of Boston University has made this valid point, and called the government deficit "a delusion" because it ignores different behavioral responses to different taxes and expenditures.

But this Social Security example is the exception, rather than the rule. In general, there will be much less than a full private offset when government saving increases. For example, suppose there is a household tax increase, and government spending is held constant. But in contrast to the Social Security case, the tax revenue is not earmarked for any specific purpose or fund. There is no particular reason why individuals should regard the tax as a substitute for private saving. Also, the tax increase is not intended to be temporary, so there is no reason for individuals to view it as a one-year aberration. Thus, there is no reason to expect individuals to cut private saving nearly as much as the increase in government saving.

However, suppose a household's tax rises $1,000, but the government promises no additional future transfer, in contrast to the Social Security case. Then it is likely that much of the tax will come out of the household's consumption, so that private saving will fall much less than $1,000. In the United States, the personal saving rate is roughly 5 percent; out of every $1,000 of current after-tax income, the average household consumes $950 and saves $50. Suppose the tax causes consumption to fall $950 and private saving to fall $50. Then when government saving rises $1,000, private saving falls only $50, so that national saving rises by $950—95 percent of the tax increase. As long as private saving falls less than $1,000, national saving will increase.

Let us summarize our response to all four objections. Each objection has merit. A NUBAR statute must plead guilty to the charge of imperfection. But the quest for the best must not be allowed to prevent achievement of the good. Despite these four objections, it remains true that a NUBAR statute will raise the national saving rate without destabilizing the economy. That should be good enough for practical reformers.

Enforcement:
The Gramm-Rudman-Hollings innovation

Suppose Congress fails to enact a budget that complies with the NUBAR statute. Then what? No matter how well a balanced budget statute is designed, it is useless if it is disobeyed.

With respect to enforcement, Gramm-Rudman-Hollings has achieved a great breakthrough: the automatic uniform spending cut to force compliance. This important innovation is as crucial for NUBAR as for the current GRH.

The significance of the automatic mechanism is this: neither the president nor legislators must go on record approving specific spending cuts. It is often said, "Isn't it a shame that Congress seems unable to vote detailed cuts to balance the budget?" It may be a shame, but it appears to be a fact. The question is, what should we do about it? It is time to recognize that politicians have an incentive to avoid spending cuts and tax increases, because both actions displease constituents. But such avoidance, of course, puts the budget in deficit and reduces our national saving rate.

Won't Congress lose control of spending priorities under a uniform mechanism? Not at all. Here's what will happen. Instead of debating whether to cut low-priority spending, Congress will instead vote to raise high-priority spending. The tentative budget on September 30 will be out of compliance. Then the automatic mechanism will uniformly cut all spending. As a result, high-priority spending will return to its original position, and only low-priority spending will be cut.

An example will illustrate. Suppose there are only two kinds of spending in the budget, L (low-priority) and H (high-priority), and spending on each is $3,000. But tax revenue is only $5,000, so total spending must be cut $1,000 to balance the budget. Suppose Congress, if forced to cut $1,000, would prefer to cut only low-priority L, and not to touch high-priority H, so that the outcome is L = $2,000 and H = $3,000. Without an automatic mechanism, this can only be done if legislators are willing to go on record as having voted to cut L by $1,000.

But with the automatic mechanism, legislators can instead leave L at $3,000, and vote to raise H to $4,500, so that on September 30, tentative planned spending is $7,500. To bring spending down to tax revenue, which is $5,000, a uniform 33 percent automatic spending cut is implemented. As a result, L ends up $2,000 and H ends up $3,000, just as the legislators desired. But each legislator can tell supporters of L that he never voted to cut L.

Thus, the automatic mechanism does not mean that Congress loses control of spending priorities. It simply enables Congress to achieve its priorities by voting to raise high-priority spending, rather than voting to cut low-priority spending. The automatic mechanism, rather than legislators, then performs the unpopular task of cutting spending so that it matches revenue.

The Supreme Court ruled that it was unconstitutional for the Comptroller General to implement the automatic uniform spending cut under GRH. But it appears that the director of the Office of Management and Budget (a presidential appointee) will be permitted to do so. If this is the case, then a NUBAR statute should contain the following provision: "If Congress's budget as of September 30 does not comply with this statute, according to the official estimate by the Office of Management and Budget, then the OMB will estimate the *uniform* percentage by which all expenditures must be cut to achieve compliance. This percentage cut shall be implemented by the director of OMB for the fiscal year that begins October 1."

Under GRH, certain categories of expenditures are exempt from the across-the-board cut. Similar exemptions could be included in NUBAR. But exemptions are really unnecessary. Congress can always increase spending in high-priority categories, as in the above example, so that the automatic cut simply restores these expenditures to the level Congress desires.

Should NUBAR be a statute
or a constitutional amendment?

Whether NUBAR is a statute or a constitutional amendment, its success depends on the automatic spending cut. Even if NUBAR were a constitutional amendment, the question would remain: What happens if Congress fails to enact a planned budget that complies with the NUBAR rule?

It seems sensible, therefore, to enact a NUBAR statute with the automatic spending cut. If it succeeds, and if Congress does not repeal the statute, then the job is done. If it succeeds, but Congress then repeals the statute, then the option of a constitutional amendment can be considered. It would be premature to give up on the statutory approach before its effectiveness has been tested.

Conclusion

A normal unemployment balanced budget rule—NUBAR—can contribute to our goal of raising the national saving rate without destabilizing the economy. However, NUBAR is not perfect. A more complicated rule may be better. And there are sophisticated objections to any balanced budget rule. But when all is said and done, NUBAR is worth enacting. Let's not allow the best to prevent the good.

Note

1. This stabilizing rule is compared to NUBAR in Laurence Seidman, "Gramm-Rudman-Hollings: Can It Be Improved?" *Challenge* 29 (July 1986), 51–54.

5

BUILD UP THE SOCIAL SECURITY FUND

My main assignment is not to strengthen Social Security, but to make sure our standard of living remains second to none. Yet wouldn't it be nice if we could do both at the same time? That's what this chapter is about. I don't want to cause you any unnecessary anxiety, but I must tell you that our Social Security system faces a little problem next century. If implemented, my proposal will help solve that problem at the same time that it immediately raises our national saving rate.

Before I begin, let's take care of this question: "Don't we already have a giant Social Security fund?" The mistake is natural. After all, every properly managed private pension does have a big fund. And the Social Security Administration tells us that it operates the Social Security Trust Fund. So it's no shame for an intelligent citizen to think that we already have a giant fund.

So what is the Social Security Trust Fund? To be blunt, until recently it has been a petty cash fund. Each year's benefits to retirees have been financed by current payroll taxes, not earnings from a giant fund. The assets of the Trust Fund have been only a tiny fraction of the liabilities to workers who have contributed. If taxes were ended, the Trust Fund would be able to pay only a tiny fraction of the benefits due these workers.

Here's my proposal. Set Social Security revenue significantly above benefits so that Social Security runs a substantial surplus each year and a large permanent Social Security fund accumulates over the next few decades. Exclude Social Security from the balanced budget statute (Gramm-Rudman-Hollings, or NUBAR described last chapter) so that the federal budget must be balanced not counting the Social Security surpluses. Finally, protect the fund from a raid.

Is my proposal novel? Not at all. Others have advocated accumulating a large permanent Social Security fund.[1] We've already begun to accumulate a genuine Social Security fund under the path-breaking Social Security reform of 1983. Unfortunately, the current buildup has three shortcomings: It is not large enough; Social Security is currently included in the Gramm-Rudman-Hollings balanced budget statute; and the fund is inadequately protected against a raid. Let me tell you about my proposals for remedying each defect.

Increase the buildup

Social Security needs a large fund buildup to handle the little problem it faces next century. You've never heard of this problem? Actually, you've probably heard a lot about it, much of it alarmist. There has been too much irresponsible fear-mongering about Social Security. The Social Security system has a problem, not a crisis. It will not collapse. You will receive a benefit when you retire. There, I hope you feel better.

But there is a problem. Why? In the absence of a large fund, each year Social Security must rely solely on current payroll tax revenue to pay benefits. The greater the revenue per retiree, the greater the benefit per retiree. So what determines whether revenue per retiree is high compared to the tax the retiree paid when he was a worker?

Two things. First, labor force growth. The more workers per retiree, the more payroll tax revenue raised per retiree. Second, real (inflation-adjusted) wage growth. The higher the wage, the more revenue raised by the payroll tax, per retiree.

Unfortunately, these two elements do not look good for the baby boomers who will be retiring in the decades near 2020. While a lot of baby boomers will reach retirement around then, there won't be as many following behind them, so that the number of workers per retiree will fall. In addition, productivity growth, which determines real wage growth, has been very low.

So what will happen without my proposal? A dramatic collapse? Not at all. Instead, Congress will either cut the Social Security "replacement rate" so that the average retiree's benefit will be a smaller fraction of his preretirement wage than it is today, or payroll tax rates will be raised several points higher than they are today. Most likely, a combination of both measures will be taken.

There will be an unpleasant intergenerational tug of war fought out in Congress, with lobbying by the old against benefit cuts, and lobbying by the young against payroll tax hikes. Congress will compromise, and neither side will be happy. There will be no collapse, but there will be much bad feeling, and much dissatisfaction with Social Security.

Two questions will naturally arise in 2020: Why do we, the retirees of 2020, deserve a replacement rate so much smaller than the retirees of 1990? And why do we, the workers of 2020, deserve payroll tax rates so much higher than the workers of 1990? Good questions. Why should Social Security treat the retirees and workers of 1990 so much differently from the retirees and workers of 2020?

The accumulation of a large Social Security fund between 1990 and 2020 is a fairer way to divide the burden between the populations of 1990 and 2020. The annual interest earnings on a large fund can help bridge the projected gap between benefits and payroll taxes in 2020, so there need not be as large a cut in the replacement rate or increase in the payroll tax rate. Today's population will bear an additional burden—releasing the revenue to build the fund—in order to reduce the burden on the population of 2020.

I suspect you are wondering why Social Security experts have not thought of this. The answer is, they have. This is exactly what the bipartisan Social Security Commission of 1982 recommended, and exactly what Congress enacted in 1983, launching the fund accumulation that is now underway.

The 1983 reform saw a problem coming, and raised both the payroll tax rate and the earnings ceiling to begin the buildup of the Social Security fund. Under that reform, the fund is projected to rise gradually to roughly 30 percent of GNP at its peak near 2020—six times annual Social Security benefits.

Not bad, you say. True enough. But then, according to projections, it will need to be drawn down to zero by 2050 because so many retired baby boomers will be entitled to benefits. So from 2020 to 2050, Social Security will significantly reduce national saving as the fund dissaves, or "decumulates."

My proposal is this: make the fund big enough so that its interest earnings are sufficient to bridge the 2020 benefits-tax revenue gap, and hence, so that the fund itself can be maintained permanently. Social Security with a permanent large fund will be a stronger Social Security. It is better for benefits to depend partly on the fund's interest earnings and partly on payroll taxes than to depend completely on payroll taxes. And Social Security will never become a source of dissaving for the economy.

Exclude Social Security
from the balanced budget statute

At present, Social Security is not excluded from the Gramm-Rudman balanced budget statute. Why not, you ask? Because, as we explained last chapter, Congress and the president have had a bit of a problem reducing the federal deficit in the 1980s. Now imagine you're a desperate Congress or president, and lo, what do you see happening in Social Security? A surplus. You think, "Wouldn't it be nice to count the Social Security surplus against the deficit in the rest of the budget so that the whole budget deficit, including Social Security, doesn't look so bad?" So Congress and the president have thus far counted Social Security toward meeting the Gramm-Rudman deficit targets.

Does this really matter? For the theme of this book, it matters crucially. Our goal is to raise national saving. To really boost national saving, we should run a surplus in the entire federal budget including Social Security. One way to do this is to run a surplus in Social Security, and a balance in the rest of the federal budget. We achieve less saving by running a surplus in the Social Security system if this is canceled by a comparable deficit (dissaving) in the rest of the federal budget.

Needless to say, Congress is not eager for you to learn that it is using Social Security surpluses to help meet its Gramm-Rudman deficit reduction targets. If you think Congress has lost its talent for smoke screens, check these shenanigans: In the 1983 Social Security Reform, Congress pledged to remove Social Security from the official ("unified") federal budget in 1993; there's nothing like giving yourself a decade to develop some discipline. Then, under a provision of the Gramm-Rudman-Hollings Balanced Budget Act in 1985, Social Security was designated an "off-budget" item in the federal budget. "Admirable," you say. Hold your praise until you read the fine print. In the very same act, Congress blithely stated that, even though Social Security is now nominally "off-budget," it still counts toward Gramm-Rudman deficit reduction targets. "Unbelievable," you say. Then it's time you showed a little respect for the creative talents of the denizens of Capitol Hill.[2]

To be fair to Congress, there is a respectable argument for keeping Social Security on-budget. In order to judge the impact of federal fiscal policy on the economy, we do need to consider all federal expenditures and revenues, including Social Security. Actually, best of all would be to keep Social Security on-budget, but then have a statute require a federal surplus, not a balanced budget.

Alas, the best is sometimes the enemy of the good. As we explained last chapter, a balanced budget target has the virtue of simplicity, and simplicity can help to discipline politicians. It is doubtful that a budget goal of an X percent surplus, instead of balance, can be made to stick. It's hard to imagine that a citizens' movement could hold Congress to achieving a budget surplus of say, 2 percent of GNP. After all, why 2 percent? But however shaky its underpinnings in theoretical economics, the goal of a balanced budget—a zero deficit—has a natural magnetism for the electorate. That reality is important for the chances of holding Congress's feet to the fire.

So, on practical grounds, it is better to move Social Security off-budget, have the statute require balance in the rest of the budget, and build the surplus within Social Security.[3] But why, you reasonably ask, should there be a better chance of achieving a surplus in Social Security than in the whole federal budget? The reason is that the baby boom retirement problem of the next century creates a tangible justification for accumulating a large Social Security fund. Without the earnings of a large fund to help bridge the projected gap between benefits and payroll tax revenues next century, either the replacement rate will be cut sharply or the payroll tax rate raised significantly. Social Security's special problem provides a justification for running surpluses that citizens and politicians can easily grasp.

How important is the fund's portfolio?

We come now to a widespread confusion about the accumulation of a genuine Social Security fund. Will the buildup raise the nation's capital stock even if the fund holds only government securities? The answer is that it will. Let me explain.

The crucial issue is whether the Social Security surplus raises the national saving rate, not what assets the fund holds. We've already said that if the Social Security surplus permits a larger deficit in the rest of the federal budget, then there is no increase in national saving. This is exactly why we urge that Social Security be excluded from the balanced budget statute.

Recall from chapter 2 that "investment equals saving" is not a theory that may be wrong; it is an accounting identity that must be true. So as long as the Social Security surplus raises the national saving rate, it will raise the nation's capital stock. How does this come about? Recall the explanation in chapter 2. An increase in the national saving rate means slower growth in consumption demand. The Federal Reserve then lowers interest rates to stimulate investment demand for machinery, equipment, and so on, so that the slower consumption growth is matched by faster investment growth. Faster investment growth means a faster increase in the nation's capital stock.

If the SS fund were to use its surplus to buy newly issued corporate stocks and bonds, everyone would agree that the surplus raises the nation's capital stock. But what happens if the surplus is used to buy government securities? The answer is that private savers, unable to obtain these government securities, will instead buy the newly issued corporate stocks and bonds. The SS fund's choice of assets will affect the private sector's portfolio. But the SS fund's portfolio decision will not undermine the increase in the nation's capital stock unless it reduces the nation's saving rate.

Should the Social Security fund be restricted to government securities? Should it hold mainly low-risk, low-return assets, or high-risk, high-return assets? These and other issues of pension fund management deserve attention. But we need not be detained here. What matters for our purpose is the raising of the national saving rate. Regardless of the fund's portfolio policy, this will be achieved if Social Security runs substantial surpluses while being excluded from the balanced budget statute.

Protecting the fund

Unfortunately, the Social Security fund that is now building up is inadequately protected from a raid. "What's a raid?" you ask. We must now speak candidly about an important practical objection to building up the Social Security fund. Imagine it is the year 2000. A healthy fund has been accumulated. It will provide an endowment that generates interest income each year that can help finance SS benefits. This endowment income will be especially important when the baby boomers retire near 2020. But the Congress of 2000 eyes the fund greedily. Why not draw down the fund now and immediately raise benefits?

Raiding of the fund will always be popular with current retirees. The key to deterring a raid is to make sure that current workers realize that it is their future benefits that are being raided. If the fund is drawn down, then its interest income will be lower in future years, and so will SS benefits. But how can millions of workers be aroused to oppose a raid?

Suppose the Social Security system is required to send each worker an annual estimate of his expected retirement benefit, based on current tax rates, benefit rules, and the size of the fund and its endowment income. A raid on the fund this year would reduce each worker's expected benefit in next year's annual statement. Every Congressman who votes for a raid would know that workers in his district will soon learn the impact of his vote on their own expected benefit. It may be somewhat abstract for a worker to learn from the media that Congress has raided the SS fund. But it is bound to be a moving, personal experience when he connects the media story to the specific dollar reduction on his annual statement.

The annual statement is a good thing in itself. Today, most workers have little idea of how much to expect from Social Security. An annual statement is worthwhile just to help people figure out how much they need to save for retirement. But the statement would also be an important obstacle to a congressional raid on the SS fund.

Where will the surplus come from?

Now we come to the unpleasant part. To achieve a surplus, Social Security taxes must be set higher than benefits. Remember that in a growing economy, taxes and benefits per person grow each year. For our purpose of raising the national saving rate, it doesn't matter whether tax growth is accelerated or benefit growth is decelerated. All that matters is that a gap is achieved, and that it is achieved without disturbing the required balance in the rest of the federal budget.

Neither faster tax growth nor slower benefit growth is likely to win any popularity awards. This should come as no surprise. The aim is to raise the national saving rate; by definition, this requires reducing the national consumption rate. That means, alas, that consumption growth must be slowed either for taxpayers or for benefit recipients. There is no escape from this somber conclusion.

While I can't offer a painless escape—there is none—I do want to note that there are many options. On the benefit side, almost no one favors a sudden cut in the absolute level of benefits. But a scheduled gradual slowdown in benefit growth may be acceptable. On the tax side, nothing says that faster tax growth must come from raising payroll tax rates. Instead, the payroll tax earnings ceiling can be raised. Perhaps more revenue can come from a tax on personal income or consumption, on business sales or value-added, or on sales of selected commodities.

The Social Security fund vs. individual funds

Why not give each worker the option of building his own fund, instead of building up a single Social Security fund? The government would provide each builder with revenue now, instead of Social Security benefits later. As long as these individual funds are excluded from the balanced budget statute, then their surpluses will raise national saving.

Of course, building many individual funds is just as painful as building one big fund. If the federal government must keep the rest of its budget balanced, then it can provide revenue to each builder only by cutting spending or raising taxes.

So which is better: a single large fund, or many individual funds? With the single fund, workers with the same wage histories will receive the same benefits. No one will enjoy an exceptional benefit, but everyone will be assured a subsistence benefit. With many individual funds, workers with the same wage histories will receive different benefits because returns will vary among funds; one fund's portfolio may soar in value, while another's may plummet. Some workers will obtain exceptional benefits; others will be destitute in old age, dependent on the welfare system for survival.

Should workers be free to risk destitution in old age? Some will say yes, others no. Before the fact, a young person may say yes. After the fact, that same person, now old, may say no. Here's my personal view. Risk-taking is good for the health of the economy—up to a point. We certainly don't want everyone guaranteed, as well as limited to, an average income. We want individuals to consider risky options, where they can strike it big, or end up well below average. On the other hand, I think we ought to discourage the all-or-none gamble played by the young person, lived by the old one.

So my preference is for a single Social Security fund where the risk is pooled and everyone is assured a minimum subsistence. Beyond that, let people take risks on private saving and career choice. But let the single Social Security fund limit the stakes for old age.

Conclusion

It is possible to advance our main objective of raising the national saving rate and to handle Social Security's 2020 problem at the same time. We can do this by running a substantial surplus each year in the Social Security system for the next few decades while excluding Social Security from the balanced budget statute. The surplus will then represent a genuine increase in national saving. Once a large permanent fund accumulates, its interest earnings will help bridge the projected gap between Social Security benefits and tax revenues when the baby boomers retire next century.

Notes

1. Martin Feldstein, "Toward a Reform of Social Security," *The Public Interest* 40 (Summer 1975), 75–95 and Lester Thurow, *The Zero-Sum Solution* (New York: Simon and Schuster, 1985), p. 250.

2. My account is based on Henry Aaron, Barry Bosworth, and Gary Burtless, *Can America Afford to Grow Old?* (Washington, D.C.: The Brookings Institution, 1989), p. 30.

3. This practical case for moving Social Security off-budget is made by Aaron, Bosworth, and Burtless, p. 122. Lawrence Summers advocates moving Social Security off-budget for the same reason in "Economic Priorities for the Next President," *Challenge* 31 (September 1988), 21–26.

6

HOW TO REDUCE
POVERTY FASTER

So far, this book has focused on how our nation can stay second to none. It's been about the United States vs. Japan and Europe. By now, I hope at least a few readers might agree that we should raise our national saving rate. But some readers may ask the following questions:

"What about the poor? Before we go running off to the international races, shouldn't we take care of poverty at home? Are the poor going to be neglected as we mobilize to stay ahead of Japan and Europe?" Wouldn't it be nice if I could answer, honestly, that many poor Americans would benefit from an attempt to stay second to none internationally, and that raising the national saving rate would reduce future poverty? It would be nice. And that's exactly what I am going to claim.

In fact, I'll go further. Raising the national saving rate is one thing you would do even if you didn't care one bit about international competition, and cared only about faster poverty reduction here at home. Will poor Americans be sacrificed so that we can stay ahead? Exactly the opposite is true. Many poor Americans will be uplifted faster if we raise our saving rate to stay ahead of Japan and Europe.

I do not claim that raising the national saving rate will single-handedly take care of our poverty problem. Poverty has neither a single cause nor a single cure. More saving today will only improve the prospects tomorrow of individuals who are able and willing to work. It cannot directly help people who are either unable, or unwilling, to work.

Nor do I claim that raising the national saving rate will necessarily raise the income of low-wage workers faster than it raises the income of other Americans. Whose income will rise faster is a complex issue I will not attempt to address. So my claim refers to "absolute poverty," not "relative poverty."

My claim is therefore modest, yet still powerful: Over the long run, faster capital accumulation is a vital weapon against absolute poverty, so raising the national saving rate should be one important component of a comprehensive anti-poverty strategy.

Faster capital accumulation:
The best anti-poverty program

In the mid–1960s, President Lyndon Johnson declared a "War on Poverty." He then proposed a set of "anti-poverty programs." Some of these programs were very good, and long overdue: Medicare for the elderly, Head Start for poor children. Nothing I am about to say should be taken as a criticism of these valuable, worthy programs.

But as a professor, I am going to emphasize one extremely harmful effect of the War on Poverty: miseducation. The War on Poverty misled the public about how most poverty really gets reduced. "Fighting poverty" became synonymous with government insurance and transfer programs. To this day, many citizens judge our commitment to poverty reduction by the intensity of support for such programs.

Common sense should tell us that these programs cannot be the main weapon against poverty, even if they have an important complementary role to play. After all, dramatic poverty reduction has been going on for two centuries in our own nation. Many Americans had risen out of poverty before Franklin Roosevelt launched his New Deal in the 1930s. And many more had done the same before Lyndon Johnson launched his War on Poverty in the 1960s.

So how did it happen? Why did the average American in the 1920s have a much higher standard of living than the average American in the 1820s? Why is the average American of the 1980s much better off than the average American of the 1920s? Why was poverty the rule two hundred years ago, but the exception today in the United States? For that matter, why is it the rule today in some countries, but the exception in others?

The answer has very little to do with government insurance and transfer programs. But it has a lot to do with the accumulation of physical, human, and knowledge capital. Once again, don't misinterpret me. Some of these government programs have made ours a more just and compassionate society. And they have reduced poverty among those unable to work. But they are simply not the lead actors in the historical drama called Poverty Reduction. It should be obvious why. Imagine a nation with very low output per person, so that consumption per person is very low, leaving the average person in poverty. Suppose that, instead of trying to raise output per person, the nation enacts a set of "anti-poverty" programs. It taxes some citizens, and makes transfers to others. Clearly, all that will happen is that poverty will be redistributed. The key to reducing poverty for the majority must be to raise output per person.

Obvious? It should be. Anti-poverty warriors should be crusaders for raising output per person. And this should lead them immediately to be hawks about capital accumulation. We should see advocates of the poor emphasizing the importance of raising our national saving rate. Some do. But unfortunately, many do not. I think it is fair to say that capital accumulation has been given little emphasis by many citizens concerned about reducing poverty.

Old Karl's mistake

So how did it happen? A dramatic story in the ascent of man

began some two hundred years ago: the industrial revolution. Today, with hindsight, it is clear that it eventually resulted in a drastic reduction in poverty. But we would do well to remind ourselves that the early reactions were, to put it mildly, mixed. The Luddites did not exactly welcome machinery. And with good reason. Here were profit-driven entrepreneurs replacing people with machines. Machines were not poverty reducers, said the Luddites, they were poverty creators. Where would it lead? Greedy capitalists would keep substituting capital for labor. Unemployment would rise, and workers would be impoverished. Incidentally, the same argument was made about "automation" in the 1960s. And many believe it today.

There is one little problem with this logic. How is it that today, with so much more machinery per person, the unemployment rate is no higher than two hundred years ago, and the average worker is so much better off? There must be a flaw in the logic. What is it?

Here's the mistake. The Luddite argument really says this: "If you're going to produce the same output, but now use more machines, then you're going to need less labor." Correct. But who says we're going to produce the same output? Suppose instead that we add machines, but keep the same labor. Then we'll get more output. And that is, in fact, what happened over the long run for the economy as a whole.

Of course, it didn't always happen in the short run at a particular factory, which is how the argument got started that machinery impoverishes workers. In the short run, the workers at a particular plant were not dreaming. Some really were laid off because of the introduction of machinery. Why? Why couldn't the employer simply keep all the workers, and raise output? Because in the short run, the market for this particular product may not have supported so large an increase in its output. So in some cases, the introduction of machinery did cause layoffs. And workers were unemployed until they could find jobs elsewhere.

To understand why it all worked out well in the end, let's consider the argument of someone who is still remembered today for predicting otherwise: good old Karl Marx. Many people think that old Karl disputed every claim made by advocates of capitalism. But this is untrue. He only took issue with the last claim: that eventually capitalism would pull workers out of poverty.

Marx fully agreed that machinery raises the productivity of workers—output per person. He conceded that profits were often saved, that saving financed investment in machinery, that machinery increased output of each worker, and that this could *potentially* enable the capitalist to raise the wage, and hence, consumption, of the average worker. But Marx denied that the wage would in fact be raised enough to enable workers to escape poverty.

Instead, he contended that the greedy capitalists would hold down the wage despite the worker's higher productivity. To be fair to old Karl, he may have conceded that some rise in the absolute wage might occur. But he insisted that the wage of workers would deteriorate relatively if not absolutely. The failure of the wage to keep pace with worker productivity would, Marx predicted, lead to less than complete happiness among the masses. You know the rest. Now at certain times and places, old Karl was right. The rise in worker productivity, made possible by machinery, was not matched by a comparable rise in the wage. But over the long haul, it is now clear that it would be hard to make a more inaccurate prediction. In fact, the real wage and consumption of today's worker in capitalist economies is dramatically higher than it was 150 years ago. The rise in worker productivity has eventually led to a significant rise in the worker's wage and standard of living.

So how did this happen? Why did the worker's wage eventually rise with his productivity? Most economists, myself included, give the following answer.

Imagine you're a profit-seeking employer back in the good old days. How do you decide how many workers to hire? Figure out the additional output, and hence, additional revenue, that another worker will give you. Compare it to the wage you must pay him. If the additional revenue exceeds the additional cost, hire him, and make the same comparison for the next worker.

Of course, as diminishing returns sets in, it eventually does not pay to hire any more at the going wage. Suppose, like a good profit-seeking capitalist, you decide to stop at the hundredth worker, because he adds only slightly more than $1 of revenue per hour, and the going hourly wage is $1.

Now you save some of your profit, and use it to invest in new machinery, which raises the productivity of your workers. Suppose that the revenue you obtain from your hundredth worker is now $2, instead of $1. In fact, you calculate that, with your new machinery, you could hire another twenty workers (for a total of 120) before diminishing returns makes another worker's revenue fall to $1.

What do you do? If the going wage is still $1, you try to hire twenty more workers. But now comes a key part of the argument. Assume that there are many other capitalists, and they are doing the same thing you are, so that they all want to hire more workers, but most workers are already employed. With only so many workers available, you can't all get what you want. At a $1 wage, the total demand for labor in the economy now exceeds the total supply. So what do you do?

Naturally, you try to bid workers away from other capitalists. You do it by offering a wage slightly above $1, say $1.10. When other workers hear of your offer, some are glad to switch. Of course, other capitalists will not sit idly by and watch their work force, and profit, disappear. Because they too have introduced machinery, they too will find it profitable to match you, and even raise you. They may raise their wage offer to $1.20, not only winning back their workers, but luring a few of yours. So now what do you do?

Remember, if necessary, you can go all the way to $2 to try to keep your original hundred workers, because your machinery has doubled the productivity of your hundredth worker. But you really don't want to do this. You would like to get all capitalists together in a room, and make a speech: "Let's not engage in a foolish wage competition. Where will it get us? Let's keep the wage at

$1, be satisfied with the same work force, and enjoy a nice profit.''

But you are a practical capitalist, and you realize that your speech won't work. Why? Because whoever cheats, and offers a slightly higher wage, will reap even more profit. Every capitalist will realize this, and everyone will be tempted to cheat. If you are foolish enough to hold the line on wages, you will simply lose your work force, and all your profit. Besides, suppose some capitalist is caught cheating. What can you do to him? Expel him from the local capitalist society? He will laugh all the way to the bank.

So you've got no choice. You've got to engage in a wage competition to hold onto your work force. So sure enough, the wage goes to $1.10, $1.20, and eventually nears $2. There it stops, because at that wage, finally, the typical capitalist does not want to expand his work force. For example, in your case, your hundredth worker adds revenue of just $2, so it wouldn't pay you to hire more than a hundred if the wage hits $2. So when the wage reaches $2, total demand for labor again matches its supply, and the wage stops rising.

You and the other capitalists shake your heads and mutter, what a shame. Oh, if only we could have kept the wage at $1, just like good old Karl said we would. You and other capitalists will probably curl up at the fireplace with a copy of good old Karl's *Das Kapital*, and try to console yourselves with the story of what was supposed to happen to the wage.

Now notice a key feature of the economist's explanation. It does not, in any way, assume that the wage rises because capitalists abandon, or even moderate, profit seeking. Just the opposite. The argument assumes that capitalists are motivated solely by profit seeking. But, it is exactly this profit seeking that makes an agreement against wage competition impractical. Sure, it would be better for all capitalists if they all stuck to the agreement. But whoever breaks it first will make even more profit in the short run. And so, with many capitalists, the agreement simply won't hold.

Of course, few economists insist that this explanation is the whole story. Sure, there were probably some capitalists who thought their workers deserved a wage increase. And there were no doubt many who liked everything about *Das Kapital* except the ending, and who therefore concluded that it might be prudent for all capitalists to raise wages. And of course, trade unions certainly played a role in raising wages at particular workplaces.

But the economist's central point is this. As long as each capitalist cares enough about his own profit to engage in wage competition, the wage will rise with productivity. So whatever raises productivity will raise the worker's wage, and reduce poverty. And it is capital accumulation that raises productivity. So capital accumulation has been, for two hundred years, *the* anti-poverty "program." It is time to recognize this fact in our public discussion about poverty reduction.

"Progressive" capital accumulation

Forget international competition over the standard of living for a moment, and imagine you are an anti-poverty warrior who now realizes that faster capital accumulation is a vital weapon. You want a higher saving rate, but this always raises a nasty question: whose consumption should grow more slowly in the short run?

As an anti-poverty warrior, you don't believe low-skilled workers can afford slower consumption growth. They live too close to the margin, which is why you want to see their wage rise faster. You surely want to exempt them from the sacrifice of slower consumption growth. So who does that leave? Unfortunately, the rest of us.

But how should the burden of slower consumption growth be allocated among the rest of us? As an anti-poverty warrior, you are sensitive to ability to pay, and probably favor progressive taxation, which puts a large share of the tax burden on the affluent. If you favor progressivity for allocating the tax burden, then you should favor it for allocating the capital accumulation burden. What distinguishes you from a run-of-the-mill capital accumulation hawk is that you favor ''progressive'' capital accumulation.

As an anti-poverty warrior who favors progressive capital accumulation, now review the policies we have set out for raising the saving rate. Of course they will all reduce poverty faster, but do they satisfy your concern for progressiveness?

Converting from the income tax to the personal consumption tax is excellent, as long as the rates are progressive. So is the buildup of the Social Security Fund, provided the revenue source is progressive. So is balancing the budget, provided the tax increase and spending cuts largely exempt low-skilled workers.

So we arrive at an important conclusion. The anti-poverty warrior and the international competitor can join forces. They can run on the same platform: faster progressive capital accumulation. And they can support the same policies: conversion to a personal consumption tax with progressive rates, budget balance, and a buildup of the Social Security Fund with progressive financing.

The earned income tax credit and last resort jobs

What else can we do to reduce poverty faster? We can raise the earned income tax credit. You've never heard of it? You're not alone. I'm sure you've heard of the minimum wage, and I know you've heard of welfare. But the earned income credit is a much better anti-poverty weapon than the minimum wage or welfare. Let me explain why.

The earned income credit (EIC) was enacted by Congress in the mid–1970s. It is a tax credit on the federal income tax. In contrast to welfare, it's available only to people who actually work. No labor earnings, no EIC. It's only available to households with children. Abandon your children, no EIC. Imagine yours is a low-earning household with children, and it is 1988. Your EIC supplement is based on your household's total labor earnings. For each $100 you earn, the government adds $14, until at $6,250 of earnings the government supplement reaches a total of $875. It remains at $875 until your income reaches $9,830. Then, to avoid paying supplements to everyone in the economy, the phase-out begins. For each additional $100 you earn, the supplement is cut $10. When your total income reaches $18,580, the supplement has been cut to zero. So if your household earns less than $18,580 of total income, you're entitled to some supplement from the government.[1] Since 1988, there has been an automatic annual increase in the maximum EIC credit and the dollar thresholds to adjust for inflation.

But what if your earnings are so low that you don't owe any federal income tax? You still can get the full EIC supplement. EIC is what is called a "refundable" tax credit. This means that if your EIC credit is greater than the tax you owe, the government will write you a check for the difference. There are two practical problems with the earned income tax credit. First, many low-income workers have never heard of it and don't realize they are eligible. The IRS has solved this problem for any household that files a tax return. It checks each return to see if the household is entitled to an EIC credit, and grants the credit even if the household has neglected to claim it. Second, some low-income households don't file a tax return. To reach them, employers should be required to notify low-wage employees that they can get an EIC check from the IRS, but only if they file a tax return. Employers should be glad to cooperate. After all, EIC makes the employer's wage more attractive to the employee.

The current EIC does have one little shortcoming: it's too meager. After all, a maximum supplement of roughly $875 in 1988 is not very much. (Remember, no one gets EIC without actually working and earning.) Fortunately, this defect can be easily corrected: Congress can substantially raise the amount.[2]

Now why is EIC better than the minimum wage? Because the minimum wage reduces employment. An employer may find it profitable to hire a low-skilled person if he can pay him $3, but not if he must pay him $5. You can pontificate all day about what employers should do. But the hard fact is that employers will offer more jobs without a minimum wage law than with one.

The EIC response is this: Let employers offer more jobs at low wages. Then provide a supplement for workers with children. This way we get the best of both worlds—more jobs, and higher incomes (wages plus the EIC supplement) for the workers with children.

The EIC is also better than the minimum wage because it is targeted. Raise the minimum wage and you raise the wage of teenagers from affluent households, while you reduce jobs for low-skilled heads of households. Raise the EIC, and you raise the money that goes only to low-earning households.

Why is the EIC better than welfare? Because it sends the right message. No work, no assistance. Abandon your children, no assistance. Of course, welfare is necessary for people genuinely unable to work. But it should be only for them. If you are capable of work, the message should be: forget welfare, but you can earn an EIC supplement by working.

What about people who genuinely want to work, but haven't been able to find a job yet, and haven't earned unemployment compensation through past work (or whose unemployment compensation has been exhausted)? Good question. The best answer is that the government should provide last resort low-wage jobs. No one will be envious of these jobs, and no one will want to stay in them any longer than they have to. But they'll provide some help until the person can find a regular private or public sector job.

Without these last resort jobs, society will be unable to stick to its message of "no work, no assistance." After all, there are some people who genuinely want to work, but can't immediately find a regular job, and may not be eligible for unemployment compensation. We can't simply turn them away, especially if they have children. But if we cave in, and make them eligible for welfare, then abuse will follow, and we won't be able to tell who really is willing to work.

The only good test of willingness to work is actual work. Last resort low-wage jobs are the key to preventing abuse. People willing to work will take them, and people unwilling to work won't. Of course, providing such jobs will cost the taxpayer some money. But preserving the message—no work, no help—is worth it.

Besides, there's plenty of useful work to be done. Many streets and parks are filthy. Carefully screened applicants can be helpers in day-care centers; in fact, this would be a good option for a responsible mother of children who are under school age, because her own children can attend the center while she earns her paycheck as an aide. If she does a good job, she may eventually obtain a regular job at the center.

Conclusion

Must we turn our backs on the poor as we gear up for the international standard of living competition? Not at all. Just the opposite is true. What is needed for the international competition is to raise the national saving rate, and this is exactly what will help reduce poverty faster. The two goals are advanced by the same policies: converting the income tax to a personal consumption tax, balancing the budget with NUBAR, and building up the Social Security Fund.

We can reduce poverty immediately by raising the earned income tax credit for households with children. The EIC is a better anti-poverty instrument than the minimum wage or welfare for people able to work. Together with last resort low-wage government jobs, the EIC sends the right message: No work, no help. It is a message taxpayers should be willing to support.

Our policies are not a panacea for all poverty. They will directly help only individuals able and willing to work. We have said nothing about how to help those unable to work, and whether or not to help those who are able but unwilling. Our task has been more modest. We claim only that these policies are vital ingredients of any effective anti-poverty strategy. And we appeal to citizens concerned about poverty reduction to give faster capital accumulation the emphasis it deserves.

Notes

1. The EIC phase-in depends on labor earnings, but the EIC phase-out depends on "adjusted gross income" (AGI) which includes capital as well as labor earnings. To obtain the EIC, you must have some labor earnings, but your AGI must be less than $18,580 in 1988.

2. Even if the household tax has been converted from income to consumption, as advocated in chapter 3, the EIC can still be implemented, because the necessary earnings data would still be included on the individual's tax return.

7

WHO SHOULD STABILIZE THE ECONOMY?

At last, it's time to talk about a little topic that is often given the spotlight in treatises on economic policy: stabilization. What do I mean by "stabilization," you ask.

I'm sure you'll agree that it's nice when the unemployment rate stays "stable" from year to year. An economy prone to sharp rises in the unemployment rate is unpleasant, not only for the people who are laid off, but also for everyone who worries that he may be laid off. An unstable unemployment rate spells immediate hardship for some, and prolonged anxiety for many. You'll recall that a severe problem along these lines developed in the 1930s.

Also, you'll surely acknowledge that it's nice when prices are relatively "stable"—in other words, if the economy has little or no inflation. At the end of the 1970s, over the course of a year, the average price rose roughly 10 percent—too fast for most people. Of course, many countries experience much higher inflation rates.

So by "stabilization" I mean keeping unemployment and prices "stable." You might well be thinking, "Aren't these the most important tasks of economic policy?" Well, maybe they are. In fact, some people think these are the only tasks. And that's one reason I didn't start this book with stabilization. Let me say a few words in explanation.

Of course stabilization is very important, but it's not everything. Suppose we keep unemployment and inflation stable. We get an A in stabilization. But we might get an F in growth, and badly lose in the international standard of living competition. How can we lose if we keep employment stable? If we employ most people to make consumer goods, and few people to make investment goods.

Here is the key point. It is possible to do an excellent job of stabilizing the economy—avoiding severe recession (high unemployment) or inflation—and do a miserable job of advancing the standard of living. If we consume most of what we produce, and do little saving and investing, then our standard of living will be static over time, even if unemployment and inflation are low.

That's why I've spent so much time emphasizing the importance of the composition of our output—how much is consumption and how much is investment—and how we use our income—how much for consumption and how much for saving. Too often these crucial issues are ignored in the fixation with avoiding severe recession or inflation.

But now that there is no danger of your missing this point, you are certainly right that we'd better take care of stabilization. If we fell into a 1930s-style depression, it wouldn't matter how we divided our shrinking pie between consumption and investment. Both would be so low that our standard of living would decline. And if we let inflation get out of control, its consequences, and the inevitable attempt to stop it, would also derail our attempt to raise our standard of living faster.

So whose job is it to stabilize the economy? I've tried to explain why it's the job of the president and Congress to meet our central economic challenge of raising the national saving rate. It is they who must decide whether to convert our income tax to a consumption tax, enact NUBAR, and build up the Social Security fund.

But what about stabilization? Maybe the best way to arrive at an answer is to look at a stabilization achievement of the early 1980s—"disinflation" (the reduction in inflation). Recall that time. A stubborn 10 percent inflation was widely declared to be "public enemy number one." Yet within a half decade, inflation had been cut more than in half and was no longer considered a serious problem. Who brought inflation down?

Who dunnit?

In 1979, with the inflation rate near 10 percent, President Carter appointed Paul Volcker to be chairman of the central bank of the United States—the Federal Reserve. Volcker and his colleagues resolved to do what was necessary to bring down inflation. They applied a "tight money" policy to the economy, long enough and hard enough, until the resulting recession brought down inflation.

Let's go through that more slowly. I'll explain what "tight money" means in a minute. But first, why does a deep recession bring down inflation? A deep recession means layoffs. Many workers become alarmed that they will lose their jobs. So instead of being aggressive at the bargaining table, unions are willing to make concessions to save jobs. Not only that. Recession also means poor profits, and employers simply can't afford large wage increases. So a deep recession slowly brings down wage increases.

Business firms set price increases to cover cost increases. When wage increases get smaller, business firms can afford to reduce price increases. And competition forces them to. Also, in a recession, market demand won't support customary price increases. So price increases get smaller. Hence, inflation declines.

The members of the Fed knew that disinflation would not be a very pleasant process. I'm sure they undertook their assignment with great regret. But there is no escaping the central point. The Fed can only bring down inflation by generating a recession. And that's precisely what it did at the beginning of the 1980s.

How did the Fed do it? By making money "tight." What does this mean? The Fed raised interest rates high enough to discourage many households and businesses from borrowing. These households and businesses were forced to cut their spending on goods and services. When producers confronted the fall in demand, they had no choice but to cut production and lay off workers.

But how does the Fed raise interest rates? Every month, unbeknownst to most of the public, the Federal Reserve's Open Market Committee—the FOMC—meets in Washington. The FOMC consists of the Fed chairman (currently Alan Greenspan, who replaced Paul Volcker), six other board members who have been appointed by the president (each term is fourteen years), and several Fed regional bank presidents. They are advised by an excellent staff of well-trained economists.

Each month the FOMC decides the stance of monetary policy—to tighten or to loosen, that is the monthly question. At the beginning of the 1980s, the FOMC almost always resolved to tighten. It told the Fed manager of open market operations in New York to cut down the purchase of government bonds. Let's see how this decision raised interest rates in the economy.

When the Fed buys bonds, the seller—a household, business firm, or governmental unit—deposits the check in its bank. The bank, in turn, obtains cash from the Fed to cover the check. Now you might think that the bank had better hold onto this cash, because, after all, it really belongs to the depositor, who could come in any old time and ask for it. But centuries ago, an early banker experienced the ecstasy of discovering that his depositors would never know if he lent out part of their cash. And by lending it, he could earn interest. So he did. And so have banks ever since.

So whenever a bank enjoys an infusion of cash, it immediately tries to lend out part of it. The more cash it has, the lower the interest rate the bank must offer to get potential borrowers to take all of it. So when the Fed cut down its purchase of government bonds at the beginning of the 1980s, less cash flowed into banks. With less cash, banks could charge a high interest rate and still find enough borrowers for their limited supply.

By cutting down its purchase of bonds, the Fed raised interest rates throughout the economy. Each month the FOMC would ask: Have we tightened enough? The question was easy to answer. If there was still no recession, then more tightening was necessary. Table 7.1 shows what the Fed was doing:

Each month, the FOMC would observe the unemployment rate. If it was still in the 7 percent range, then the Fed would take the interest rate up, and wait a month to observe again. The borrowers and spenders in the economy held out gallantly as the prime rate (the interest rate banks charge their most favored customers) rose to unprecedented heights. Finally, in late 1981, the Fed won its battle, and many potential borrowers and spenders surrendered. Confronted with record interest rates, they at last cut down their borrowing and spending. The economy fell off a cliff into the worst recession since the 1930s as the unemployment rate rose sharply in 1982. In the worst month of 1982, the unemployment rate nearly reached 11 percent, and it averaged 9.5 percent for the year.

Table 7.1 also shows that the severe recession succeeded in bringing down inflation. Just in time, in mid–1982 the Fed relented, let interest rates come down, and prevented the recession from becoming a depression. In fact, a recovery began in 1983 (though it is still not evident in the unemployment rate), and was running at full steam in 1984. Since then, the Fed has done a good job of keeping the unemployment rate near normal, and the inflation rate low.

Should the Fed have done it? Most economists agree that inflation had to be brought down. Some would have preferred a milder recession that lasted longer to the sharp, severe recession that occurred. But most concede that it is difficult for the Fed to "fine-tune" a slowdown of the economy. It is possible that most FOMC members would also have preferred a milder, longer recession.

Could the Fed have used any help? A minority of economists think a wage-price policy could have helped the Fed bring down inflation with less recession by applying some direct pressure to firms to reduce price increases. The majority of economists dis-

Table 7.1

	Unemployment rate (percent)	Prime interest rate (percent)	Inflation rate (percent)
1977	6.9	6.83	6.7
1978	6.0	9.06	7.3
1979	5.8	12.67	8.9
1980	7.0	15.27	9.0
1981	7.5	18.87	9.7
1982	9.5	14.86	6.4
1983	9.5	10.79	3.8

agree and think a wage-price policy would have been ineffective. In any case, it's now water under the bridge. Inflation is down, and almost all economists agree that it's up to the Fed to keep it that way.

So let's summarize: The Fed intentionally caused the recession of 1982 and the reduction in inflation that accompanied it. The two went together. Without the recession, there would have been no disinflation. And the Fed generated both.

Miseducation by politicians

But you would never know "who dunnit" if you listened to the rhetoric of the two political conventions of 1984 or 1988. The Republicans praised President Reagan for conquering inflation, but regarded the recession of 1982 as an irrelevant natural disaster, akin to an earthquake. The Democrats blamed the president for causing the worst recession since the 1930s, but regarded the disinflation as a mysterious natural blessing, akin to a fortuitous change in the climate. Economists could only sit in front of their TV sets and watch helplessly as millions of Americans were miseducated about recent economic history. How had inflation been brought down? The Republicans cheerfully told the media, "The president's policies." Which policies, exactly? The media (with a few exceptions) never asked, and the Republicans never said.

Well, that's not quite true. The best of the Republicans never said, because they knew that talking about the Fed's recession was not likely to win votes, so rather than distort any further, they just repeated, "The president's policies," and left it at that. Unfortunately, there were other Republicans who went further. They said, "The president's historic tax cut brought down inflation."

Now the temptation is understandable. After all, to the general public, the president's most famous economic policy was surely the income-tax cut he proposed, and persuaded Congress to enact, in 1981. So why not claim that the tax cut did it? Indeed, such a claim would be widely believed for the unfortunate reason that most of the public has not had the opportunity to study any economics.

But few things drive economists wilder than the claim that the tax cut of 1981 brought down inflation. If you took a survey of economists of all political persuasions, there would be near unanimity that it was the tight money policy of the Fed that generated both the severe recession and the resulting reduction in inflation. Don't misunderstand. Many (though not all) conservative economists supported the tax cut of 1981. But not to bring down inflation. For example, Milton Friedman, dean of "monetarist" economists, supported the tax cut because, as a conservative, he wanted to reduce the size of government. But Friedman, who has devoted much of his career to emphasizing the importance of money in the determination of inflation, would be near apoplexy should someone claim that the tax cut of 1981 brought down inflation.

Now what about the Democrats? They claimed that "Reaganomics" had caused the worst recession since the 1930s. But which policies, exactly? They never said. Well, once again, that's not quite true. The best of the Democrats never said, because then it would come out that the Fed did it to reduce inflation. And worse yet, they would have to admit that their own president, Jimmy Carter, had appointed Fed chairman Volcker in 1979, so that if any president were indirectly responsible, it was a Democratic president. So the best of the Democrats just said,

"Reaganomics," and let it go at that.

But unfortunately, some Democrats went further. Once again, the temptation is understandable. Since President Reagan's most famous economic policy was his tax cut, these Democrats hinted that the president's tax cut caused the worst recession since the 1930s. Few could get themselves to literally say that the tax cut caused the recession. But they would say, "The tax cut was a great mistake. Look what happened. We got the worst recession since the 1930s." Now if there is anything that drives economists wilder than the claim that the tax cut brought down inflation, it is the claim that the tax cut caused the recession. How in God's name can a tax cut cause a recession? A tax cut leaves more cash in people's pockets and raises their spending on goods and services, thereby stimulating production and employment—the opposite of recession.

As for the 1982 recession, there is also a small timing problem. The tax cut was enacted in 1981 to go into effect in 1982. But as Table 7.1 indicates, the economy plunged into recession before the tax cut took effect. In fact, the tax cut contributed to the recovery that began in 1983 as a result of the Fed's shifting gears in mid–1982.

So why were the politicians of both parties able to mislead the public? While our nation certainly has some reporters with excellent training in economics, unfortunately many reporters who cover politics have not had the opportunity to study economics, and naturally shy away from asking questions like, "Mr. Republican, exactly how did the tax cut reduce inflation?" or "Mr. Democrat, exactly how did Reaganomics cause the recession?"

The Fed's target

What must the Fed do to stabilize the economy, to keep unemployment and inflation on target and relatively constant? Before answering this question, we must check something immediately. Are our two goals compatible? If unemployment is "on target," will inflation stay constant?

Experience over the past three decades seems to suggest that if the U.S. economy is run near a particular unemployment rate—about 6 percent currently—then the inflation rate usually stays roughly constant. If the unemployment rate is much below this particular value, then inflation usually rises; and if the unemployment rate is much above this particular value, then inflation usually falls. For example, in the late 1960s, the unemployment rate was near 4 percent, and inflation rose. In the 1982 recession, the unemployment rate exceeded 9 percent, and inflation declined, as we saw in Table 7.1.

So if we accept the hypothesis that the economy has a "constant-inflation" unemployment rate, or CIRU (pronounced "see-roo"), and if we accept this CIRU as our unemployment rate target, then our two goals are compatible. Incidentally, many economists call the CIRU the "natural rate of unemployment." I prefer "CIRU," to emphasize the point that if the economy is at this unemployment rate, the inflation rate usually stays constant. There is considerable uncertainty about the numerical value of the CIRU. During most of the 1980s, the CIRU appeared to be near 7 percent.[1] Today, it may be closer to 6 percent. I will use the value 6 percent in my examples.

Why does inflation usually rise if the economy is below the CIRU? A low unemployment rate raises the relative bargaining strength of workers. The fear of layoffs diminishes, and unions become more aggressive. Employers have difficulty finding workers, and are afraid of losing workers through stingy wage increases. Moreover, a low unemployment rate usually means that businesses are enjoying high revenues and profits, so they can afford higher wage increases. Thus, a low unemployment rate usually results in a rise in wage increases, cost increases, and price increases—that is, a rise in inflation.

Just the reverse is true if the economy has a high unemployment rate. A high unemployment rate reduces the relative bargaining strength of workers. The fear of layoffs rises, and unions become more timid. Employers have no difficulty finding workers, and have no fear of losing workers through stingy wage increases. Moreover, a high unemployment rate usually means that businesses are suffering low revenues and profits, so they are forced to reduce wage increases. Thus, a high unemployment rate usually results in a fall in wage increases, cost increases, and price increases—a fall in inflation.

So the Fed's task is to keep the unemployment rate near the CIRU, and inflation steady at a low rate. The goals are compatible, but you undoubtedly have one question: must we really settle for a 6 percent unemployment rate? Fortunately, the answer is no. We can do better. But the Fed can't. The Fed can't reduce the CIRU (the unemployment rate at which inflation usually stays constant). The Fed's job is simply to try to keep the economy near the current CIRU. Someone else will have to lower the CIRU. I promise to tell you who, and how, before this chapter ends.

Back to the Fed's challenge. Imagine for a moment that inflation is zero, and unemployment is at the CIRU—roughly 6 percent. How can the Fed keep it that way? If output per worker—labor productivity—grows 2 percent per year due to capital accumulation and technological change, then the same number of workers can produce 2 percent more output next year. So if real output grows 2 percent, the unemployment rate will stay at 6 percent if the labor force—the number who want to work—remains constant. If the labor force grows 1 percent instead of staying constant, then real output must grow 3 percent to keep the unemployment rate at 6 percent. I will call the sum of productivity growth and labor force growth "normal real output growth." In this example, normal real output growth is therefore 3 percent (2 percent plus 1 percent).

The Fed's job is to make total dollar spending in the economy rise 3 percent per year. If it does, there will be enough demand to buy 3 percent more real output, provided prices stay constant. And if real output rises 3 percent, then the unemployment rate will stay at 6 percent. And if the unemployment rate is 6 percent, then experience shows that inflation should stay steady, at zero, and prices will remain roughly constant.

So if the Fed wants a zero-inflation economy with the unemployment rate at the CIRU, it must try to keep the growth rate of total spending equal to normal real output growth—3 percent in this example. However, the Fed may be less ambitious. It may settle for a steady 4 percent inflation rate. If so, then its task is to keep the growth rate of total spending at 7 percent, so that 4 percent of the spending goes for price increases, and 3 percent for an increase in real output.

We can summarize: The Fed's target is to achieve a growth rate of total spending equal to normal real output growth plus the desired inflation rate. Since normal real output growth is roughly 3 percent, the Fed's normal target should be a growth rate of total spending not much greater than 3 percent.

The great offsetter

How can the Fed meet its target for total spending growth? The answer is that the Fed is the great offsetter. Its job is to assess the other forces influencing total spending in the economy, and to lean against the wind.

Suppose the Fed estimates that household and business psychology, and government budget policy, will all tend to make spending grow too slowly in the months ahead. Then the Fed's job is to stimulate spending. How? By reducing interest rates. How? By injecting more cash into the banking system. How? By buying more government bonds in the open market.

Recall again how this works. When the Fed buys government bonds, the sellers—households, businesses, and governmental units—deposit Fed checks at their banks. The banks, in turn, obtain cash from the Fed to cover the checks. The banks then seek borrowers so that they can earn interest on part of this cash. The more bonds the Fed buys, the more cash the banks obtain, and the lower the interest rate they must offer to induce potential borrowers to take all the cash they seek to lend.

So to stimulate more borrowing and spending in the economy, the Fed simply raises its "open market" purchases of government bonds. It does just the reverse if it wants to reduce the growth of spending in the economy.

Of course, hitting it just right is no simple task. I don't want to give the false impression that the Fed can fine-tune the growth of total spending. After all, it's hard to guess at consumer and business psychology. Currently, it's difficult to guess what government budget policy will be. And even if the Fed knew these precisely, it could not be sure exactly how much to adjust its bond purchases because the link between money injection and the fall in interest rates and rise in spending is imprecise.

So we can't expect perfection from the Fed. But the Fed is often able to do a pretty good job. Its excellent technical staff uses the best econometric models—economic models based on statistical analysis of U.S. economic data—to try to estimate the bond purchases that will keep total spending growth on target. And it continuously adjusts its open market operations based on new data.

The Fed has controlled the economy fairly well during the 1980s. Remember, it engineered the 1982 recession in order to bring down inflation. Since then it has kept spending growth near its target, so that the unemployment rate has stayed near 6 percent, real output growth has stayed near 3 percent, and the inflation rate has stayed steady near 4 percent.

Now, I am well aware of the snickering that goes on about economic forecasting. And I think this is the right moment to say my piece about it.

First of all, much of the public seems to think that most economists are forecasters, so that economics can be judged by its forecasting accuracy. A gross misconception! Most economists spend no time forecasting. So what do we do for a living? We develop theories and models, and perform empirical studies with actual data, to help us understand how the economy actually works and to guide the development of policies like the ones that have been set out in this book. Flip the pages of this book. Where's the forecasting? This book is built on the research that occupies the time of most economists—research that has nothing to do with forecasting.

Second, it's true that some economists work on short-term

forecasting. Among these forecasters, a few promise too much, and deserve the snickering they get. But most forecasters don't promise too much. They promise only to use the best techniques available and to do the best they can.

Common sense should tell anyone that forecasters can't be on target all the time for a simple reason: ours is not a totalitarian economy. You are free to change your mind, at this very moment, about what you will buy today. So is every other consumer. And so is every business. Everyone is free to react to the latest economic and political news any way he wants. So in a free economy, how can forecasters always be on target?

The goal of responsible forecasters is more modest. While you are free to change your mind today, you are constrained by your actual wealth and income. So there are limits to what you can do. The same is true of every business manager. It is these objective constraints on which forecasters concentrate. And, remarkably, models based on these constraints often do a decent job of forecasting.

So, ye snickerers, if you want highly accurate forecasting, surrender your freedom. Let the government decide your spending, and forecasting will surely improve. But if you want to keep the freedom to change your minds from day to day, then hold your tongues. Have the decency to admit that no one can forecast you perfectly, precisely because you are free.

Back to the Fed's task. Suppose we phase in a policy that raises household saving. For example, we gradually convert from the income tax to the consumption tax. What must the Fed do? The Fed will anticipate, and soon observe, a slowdown in the growth of consumer spending. It must therefore act in advance to reduce interest rates in order to stimulate investment spending. As the policy phases in, the Fed will raise its purchase of government bonds, inject more cash into the banking system, and the result will be a fall in interest rates and a rise in borrowing by business firms to finance real investment in plants and equipment.

Thus, the Fed will offset the slower growth in consumer spending by stimulating faster growth in investment spending. If the

Fed hits it just right, the result will be to keep total spending growth on target. But the composition of this growth will have been changed to faster investment growth and slower consumption growth.

This may strike some readers as a delicate operation. It is. But it is no more delicate than the one the Fed performs every day. Whether we implement our policy or not, the economy is continuously subject to changes in spending that the Fed must offset in order to keep it stable. One day the stock market rises. The next day it falls. The Fed must try to offset the effects on household and business spending. So handling a new policy is nothing special, as long as the policy is phased in gradually.

Our policy proposals, therefore, always assume that the Fed will play the role of the great offsetter. The Fed cannot perform this role perfectly in a free economy; nevertheless, it usually performs it remarkably well.

Should the president and Congress try to help?

The president and Congress, not the Fed, hold the key to raising the national saving rate. If you think back on the policies proposed in this book, you'll see that they've got plenty to do. There's no danger that they will wilt offstage if they leave stabilization to the Fed. And "leave it to the Fed" is just what they should do.

Actually, there is one step the president and Congress can take when it comes to stabilization. They can avoid destabilizing fiscal actions that make the Fed's job much tougher. The best way to do this is to lock themselves into neutrality and predictability by enacting the NUBAR balanced budget statute. Recall that the goal of NUBAR is modest. It keeps the federal budget neutral. It prevents shifts in the budget that would make a recession or inflation worse. It prevents destabilization due to government fiscal (budget) policy.

NUBAR would also make government fiscal policy predictable. At last, the Fed would know what the federal budget position would be. And this would make it easier for the Fed to conduct an effective monetary policy. The Fed still could not be sure what the private sector's spending would be. But at least it would have a better idea about government spending and taxes.

Now why shouldn't the president and Congress be more ambitious? Why shouldn't they try to actively stabilize the economy, rather than simply adhering to a rule such as NUBAR, and leaving the Fed to do the rest? True, the president and Congress do have the power to raise and lower spending in the economy. The Fed does it by moving interest rates. The president and Congress could do it by changing the taxes people pay, or by changing the government's own spending. In theory, the president and Congress could even stabilize the economy without the Fed's help.

The problem is not with theory, but with practice. Two historical examples will make my point. In the early 1960s, many economists believed that the unemployment rate was unnecessarily high, and that a tax cut should be used to stimulate the economy. So a tax cut was enacted and, along with an expansionary monetary policy, it helped reduce the unemployment rate. But in the mid-1960s, the buildup in military spending for the Vietnam War resulted in excessive spending, thereby threatening to push the unemployment rate below the CIRU, thereby raising inflation.

In theory, the answer was simple. Just as the president and Congress had stimulated private spending by cutting taxes, now they must restrain spending by raising taxes. In theory, symmetry was easy. But in practice, it was not. Chairman of the Council of Economic Advisers Gardiner Ackley told President Johnson that a tax increase was required to prevent inflation. President Johnson, however, decided that the last thing he needed was to ask the American people for a tax increase to help finance the military buildup. So he delayed for two years, and by then inflation had already risen substantially.

Now to my second example, which we've already discussed. At the beginning of the 1980s, the country cried out for disinflation. The Fed rose to the challenge, and applied the painful medicine of a tight money recession until disinflation was achieved. Now what did the president and Congress do during this period when the economy badly needed restraint?

You guessed it. They enacted a sweeping tax cut and raised spending as a fraction of GNP, thereby stimulating the economy. Luckily, their brave actions hit the economy after the Fed had generated the deep recession and disinflation, so that the fiscal stimulus helped begin the recovery. But to credit them with wisdom, rather than luck, would be ludicrous.

Let me put it this way. Suppose it had been up to Congress and the president alone to generate the recession and disinflation. Suppose we had relied on them to get the job done by raising taxes and cutting spending enough to slow total spending in the economy. Is there any doubt that they would have failed, and our inflation problem would have persisted, or even gotten worse? After all, they still can't get close to planning a balanced budget.

So what lessons should we draw from these episodes? Some economists conclude that we should redouble our efforts to teach politicians to practice symmetrical fiscal policy. They must be taught to vote promptly for tax increases and spending cuts when the economy needs slower spending. But I draw another conclusion. Let's face it. Congressmen and senators are never going to go cheerfully on record voting for tax increases and spending cuts; and few presidents propose such austerity in the first place. If they are willing to do so at all, it is after months of delay. So if we let them vote every few months, they will inevitably practice asymmetrical policy. They will gladly cut taxes and raise spending when we ask for stimulus, but they will strangely lose their ability to hear us when we call for restraint.

By contrast, the Fed can engineer restraint when restraint is needed. Why? Not because the Fed is necessarily wiser than Congress and the president, but because it is more insulated from political and popular pressure. First of all, much of the public has never heard of the Fed. How many people understand how the Fed influences the fluctuations of the economy? Second, the members of the Fed Open Market Committee don't run for office every two, four, or six years.

Consider this scene from mid–1982. It's a dinner party in suburban Washington D.C. But instead of cheer, there is gloom and tension around the table. As one guest empties his wine glass for the sixth time, he whispers to his neighbor that his business is about to go under, ruined by the worst recession since the 1930s.

"That son of a –– in the White House will never get my vote again. And the whole damned Congress should be drowned in the Potomac," he mutters in anguish. Then he asks his neighbor, "And what do you do?"

"I'm a banker," comes the reply. All around the dinner table, denunciations of the president and Congress can be heard. One man has lost his job, but no one knows it. Several others fear for theirs. Only the banker seems calm.

With good reason. Not only is his job secure. What no one at the dinner party knows is that he is no ordinary banker. In fact, he has been a member of the Fed's Open Market Committee for several years. His monthly votes have generated the recession that has caused the immediate pain around the table. The resulting disinflation will set the stage for a strong recovery that will last for the rest of the decade. But the pleasure of that recovery is still in the future. Perhaps as he voted, he was strengthened by the knowledge that no one in his social circle would ever know his role or responsibility.

Now anyone who believes in democracy must have mixed feelings about such a dinner party scene. It is troubling that symmetrical stabilization policy, necessary for the long-run health of the economy, seems to depend on insulation from popular and political pressure. But after all, isn't this the reason we try to insulate the Supreme Court?

So we have two choices. We can exhort Congress and the president to be courageous, and count on them to vote for fiscal medicine when it is medicine we need; or we can face political reality, and be thankful that we have another option: count on the Fed.

If we decide to count on the Fed, then what should we want

from Congress and the president? Simply, that they tie their own hands so they can't do harm. They can do this by enacting a NUBAR balanced budget statute. Every year, the planned budget must be estimated to be balanced on the assumption that the unemployment rate will be normal (the average of the preceding decade) in the coming fiscal year. If the tentative planned budget has an estimated deficit, then an automatic uniform spending cut gets it into compliance at the start of the fiscal year. No one must ever go on record voting for painful spending cuts. Yet the job gets done.

So my request to Congress and the president is simply this: Enact a NUBAR statute, and then leave stabilization to the Fed.

Something Congress and the president can do

There is one thing that Congress and the president can do. In contrast to stabilization, it is something the Fed can't do. Congress and the president can and should reduce the constant-inflation unemployment rate (CIRU) of the economy through structural policies.

Remember that I told you earlier in this chapter that we can do better than a 6 percent unemployment rate—roughly the value of the current CIRU. I promised to tell you how. Let me make good on my promise.

First, why can't the Fed do it? The Fed can inject more money into the economy through its open market operations; it can reduce interest rates, stimulate spending, and temporarily reduce the unemployment rate below 6 percent. But the trouble is, this will set inflation rising. And as long as the Fed pumps in enough money to keep the unemployment rate below 6 percent, inflation will keep on rising. So eventually, to prevent inflation from getting completely out of control, the Fed will be forced to retreat and let the unemployment rate come back up to 6 percent.

The only way to permanently bring unemployment below 6 percent is to reduce the CIRU itself—the unemployment rate at which inflation stays constant. But how can this be done? The answer is, not by monetary and fiscal policies that affect total spending in the economy, but by structural policies that influence the labor market.

It so happens we already met these structural policies in our discussion of poverty reduction. Recall that I championed the earned income tax credit (EIC), not the minimum wage, to help the working poor. There I stressed the impact of the EIC on the incomes of low-wage workers. Now I'll emphasize its impact on the CIRU.

One reason that the current CIRU is so high—perhaps 6 percent—is that it is unprofitable for businesses to hire some low-skilled persons except at very low wages. The minimum wage law prevents such wages from being offered. But even without the minimum wage, many low-skilled persons would refuse the jobs because the work would leave them in poverty. Instead, some turn to welfare. A few turn to crime. Many remain unemployed, searching for a higher-paying job.

A generous EIC would change this unhappy situation. Recall how it works. If you don't work, you get no government supplement. But for each $100 you earn, the government will supplement $X. Today, $X is $14, but a more generous EIC would make $X larger. With a generous EIC, low-skilled persons could afford to take low-wage jobs because the wage plus the government supplement would provide enough income to support a family.

The EIC is our carrot. Also recall our stick. A low-wage job, such as cleaning streets or parks, or helping in day-care centers, would be guaranteed by the government. Welfare would be ended for persons able to work. So low-skilled persons would have to switch from welfare to work, preferably to a regular job aided by the EIC supplement, but if necessary to the guaranteed job.

These structural labor market policies would reduce the CIRU of the economy. And only Congress and the president, not the Fed, can enact them.

A division of labor

So let each do the task he is suited to do. Who should try to keep the unemployment rate near the current CIRU, and inflation steady and low? Our good old central bank, the Federal Reserve. What should the president and Congress do about stabilization? Enact a NUBAR balanced budget statute, which will keep them from destabilizing the economy, and then leave stabilization to the Fed.

Who should reduce the CIRU with structural labor market policies? The president and Congress. They can do it by making the earned income tax credit more generous, and replacing welfare with a guaranteed low-wage job for persons able to work.

If each sticks to his proper assignment, the whole job can be nicely done.

Note

1. The use of data to estimate the CIRU is explained in chapter 6 of my textbook *Macroeconomics* (San Diego: Harcourt, Brace, Jovanovich, 1987).

8

SAVING AND
INTERNATIONAL TRADE

The time has come to return to Adam and Eve. Recall that when we left them at the end of chapter 1, they were in a state of high anxiety. Adam had wandered Far East of Eden, come upon the J island, climbed Mount Fuji, and to his horror, discovered couple J planning to save enough for two tractors. He had raced home to Eden with the shocking news.

Recall that before Adam's discovery of the J's, our Eden couple had decided not to save for a tractor. Since the Beginning, they had lived without tools, producing and consuming $100 worth of food per year. To build a tractor, they would need to cut food production by $40 in the year of construction. Thereafter, it is true, they would be able to produce and consume $120 per year, but Adam pleaded with Eve that the initial sacrifice was too great. And so they had decided not to do it.

On Adam's return home from the J island, our Eden couple swallowed the bitter conclusion that their world had changed forever. Could they live without a tractor when the J's had two? Could they give their children a lower standard of living than the J's? No they couldn't, they decided. And so it seemed that they too would have to save for a tractor. At least, that's where we left them. But all that night Adam tossed and turned, trying to escape the nightmare of saving. Just as dawn broke, his turbulence ended, and a pacific grin came over his sleepy face. Suddenly, he awoke with feverish excitement and shook Eve.

"We don't have to save! We don't have to save!" he shouted ecstatically.

"What do you mean?" asked Eve sleepily.

"We can borrow from the J's to finance a tractor," Adam exclaimed with joy. "If we borrow, we can have our tractor, and we won't have to cut our consumption below $100 in the year we acquire it!"

"So," said Eve, "you think that our solution is simply to borrow from J-Land?"

"Well, isn't it?" asked Adam, suddenly growing worried.

"Poor dear," said Eve.

There's just no substitute for our own saving

"Adam, my love, sit down and have some breakfast. This is one lecture you don't want to hear on an empty stomach."

Adam ate nervously, and then Eve began.

"Suppose that the quantity and quality of land and labor are the same in Eden and J-Land. But suppose we save nothing this year, and the J's save for two tractors. If our two economies were isolated, then beginning next year, obviously two tractors would operate in J-Land, and none in Eden, so J-Land's output would be greater than Eden's.

"But," continued Eve, "suppose our two economies interact. Then I will show you, in a moment, why one of the two tractors would be invested in Eden. In fact, in future years, output in J-Land and Eden would be identical, because both economies would have one tractor."

"Yes!" shouted Adam. "That's what I was hoping!"

"Adam, my love, don't celebrate too soon. Let me continue. Remember we said that the rate of return on one tractor would be 50 percent, because it costs $40, but raises output $20 per year. Well that's true whether it operates in J-Land or Eden. But if a second tractor is used in J-Land, then the return on the second will be less—for example, 40 percent."

"Why?" asked Adam.

"The reason, Adam, is simple. The first tractor will work the best land in J-Land. If a second tractor also operates in J-Land, it will work land that is not quite as fertile, so its return will be less. I call this phenomenon 'diminishing returns'—remind me to emphasize it when I write my economics textbook.

"But," Eve continued, "if the second tractor is used in Eden, we'll use it to work our best land, and its return will be 50 percent. So if the second tractor is invested in Eden, instead of J-Land, it will yield a higher return—50 percent instead of 40 percent. Now, Adam, suppose for a moment you were the J's, and you were willing to save $80. Would you use your $80 to finance two tractors in J-Land? Or would you use your $80 to finance one tractor in J-Land and one in Eden?"

"Why, the answer is obvious even to me," exclaimed Adam. "I'd split my $80 between one tractor in each country, because then each $40 would earn a 50 percent return. If I put all $80 into tractors in J-Land, the first $40 would earn a 50 percent return, but the second $40 would only earn a 40 percent return."

"I'm proud of you," said Eve. "To obtain the higher return, the J's will lend us $40 to obtain one tractor for use in Eden. Thus, in future years, both economies will operate with one tractor, and use it to work its best land, so our output and J-Land's will be identical."

"But," Adam said, "I'm still shaky on the mechanics of how saving in J-Land finances investment in Eden."

"Of course," replied Eve patiently. "Let's elaborate our ritual."

She led Adam to the two boulders, and reminded him that one was a bank.

"This bank," Eve explained, "would receive all saving, and lend it to investors to purchase tractors. In the year when saving and investment occur, both economies produce $100 of output and income. We save nothing, and the J's save $80—enough to finance two tractors, $40 each. The J's bring $80 of saving to the bank. The bank lends it out to whoever can use it to generate the highest return."

"Why does the bank care about who can generate the highest return?" asked Adam.

"Because, my love," Eve replied, "the bank will charge interest on the loan to the borrowers, and the higher the return on the investment, the higher the interest the bank can collect. The J savers, of course, will ultimately receive this interest.

"Now," Eve continued, "imagine that you and I go to the bank as investors seeking to borrow $40 to buy a tractor, and J investors with the same motive come to the bank as well. On the first tractor, we and the J's will each generate a 50 percent return. Let me assume, to keep things simple, that the owners of land and labor are unable to capture any of this 50 percent return. Then the bank can charge us interest of just under 50 percent, and we will still find it worth borrowing, because the return on the tractor will slightly exceed the interest we must pay the bank. But J investors who seek a second tractor will find the interest rate too high, because they can generate only a 40 percent return on the second tractor. So we will get the loan, not them."

"I feel sorry for the J's," Adam laughed. "We save nothing, they save $80 for two tractors, and yet one tractor gets invested and used in both economies, so that we can produce the same output as they can in future years. Thrift is folly."

"Ah, Adam, I'm afraid you've missed the crucial point. Let's go a step further. Just as the tractor is 'permanent' and never wears out (recall that God has not yet cursed mankind with depreciation), so that a $40 tractor raises output by $20 in every future year, let's assume that the bank is willing to give us a permanent loan that 'never wears out,' so that we never have to repay the principal—the $40—but must pay a constant amount of interest in every future year. Having permanently borrowed $40, in each future year we will owe the bank nearly $20 per year of interest, because the bank's interest rate is just under 50 percent. Who do you think will ultimately receive this interest? The J's, who saved in the initial year. In all future years, interest payments will flow from Eden to J-Land through the bank.

"Let's suppose," Eve continued, "that there is no further saving by anyone in future years. Both economies will produce the same output—$120 per year of food—because the $40 tractor has raised output from $100 to $120 in both economies. But although one tractor is used in each economy, in effect the J's own both tractors. Because of their saving in the initial year, they receive the return from both tractors. Thus, we will continue to consume only $100, because we must pay $20 of interest to the J's, through the bank, while the J's will consume $140 per year— the $120 they produce in J-Land, plus the $20 they can buy with our interest payments."

At last Adam seemed to follow Eve's analysis. "If someone looked at our two economies in future years," he said, "they might think we have the same standard of living because we each use one tractor, so our machinery per worker is the same, and our output per worker—our labor productivity—is the same. But they would be mistaken."

"Exactly right," said Eve. "What counts is who owns the capital equipment—the tractors. The J's own both tractors even though each economy uses one in production. Thus, the J's have a 'wealth' of $80, and we have no wealth. As a result, the J's wealth generates $40 of capital income, a 50 percent return on their wealth. Both we and the J's earn $100 of labor income, but the J's earn $40 of capital income. Thus, the J's total income is $140 while ours is $100, and in future years, their consumption will be $140, while ours will be $100."

Eve continued. "Wealth is 'net worth.' We possess $40 of assets—one tractor—but our liabilities are also $40 because we borrowed $40 from J-Land; so our net worth (assets minus liabilities) is zero. By contrast, the J's net worth is $80. They possess a $40 tractor, and they are also owed $40 by us. In fact, we will give them a $40 Eden bond to hold to indicate this, so their total assets are $80. With zero liabilities, their net worth is $80. Hence, our wealth is zero, and theirs is $80. And the difference in wealth is, of course, due to the difference in saving.''

"So," continued Adam, "we would be in debt to J-Land. We would be a debtor nation, because our wealth—zero—would be less than our capital stock—$40. And J-Land would be a creditor nation, because its wealth—$80—would exceed its own capital stock—$40. So every year, debtor nation Eden would make interest payments of $20 to creditor nation J-Land.''

"That's right," replied Eve.

"Then," concluded Adam, "what matters for our future standard of living is the saving we do, not the investment that occurs within our borders.''

"I'm proud of you," exclaimed Eve. "Suppose we tried to ignore the fact that the J's saved $80 and we saved nothing. We might try to defend ourselves by pointing out that investment was $40 in both economies. Each country obtained one tractor. Then, in future years, we could point out that both economies produced $120 of output. But, in fact, their standard of living would be higher, because they would have more wealth, receive interest payments from us, and therefore would afford more consumption.''

"I have one last question," said Adam with new confidence. "One $40 tractor raises output $20 per year—a 50 percent return. You assumed that the J savers will capture the full return, so that we will pay them a 50 percent interest rate, or $20 per year. But isn't it possible they will capture only a fraction of the 50 percent return, so that we will capture a fraction ourselves? For example, maybe we will only pay them 25 percent (not 50 percent) of $40, or $10 per year, and keep $10 per year for ourselves.''

"I have a confession," said Eve. "You are right. *If* the tractor raises the *marginal* product (the increment in output due to the *last* increment of labor and land) of our labor and land, then we will capture a fraction of the return, so the outcome won't be so bad. I'll explain why, any day you are willing to hear a lecture on the marginal productivity theory of income distribution.

"But," continued Eve, "my simplification is justified because it doesn't change the basic point. If they save and we don't, then even if the J's capture only a fraction of the full return, their future standard of living will still exceed ours. The reason is simple. The J's, who own all labor, land, and capital used in J-Land, will obviously capture the full return on the $40 tractor invested in J-Land. And as long as J savers capture some of the return on the $40 tractor invested in Eden, we will capture only a fraction of the full return. So due to the two tractors, the J's future standard of living must be higher than ours, even if we capture a fraction of the return on our $40 tractor.''

Trade between Eden and J-Land

Adam looked glum. Finally, he said, ''Eve, I understand that what really matters is that the J's will accumulate more wealth than we do if they save and we don't, but I'm curious about what would happen to exports and imports.''

''Let's trace it through,'' said Eve. ''In the year of saving and investment, assume one tractor is built in each economy, so each economy produces $60 of food, and a $40 tractor. But we borrow $40 from J savers through the bank. We use the $40 to keep our consumption at $100, while the J's reduce their consumption to $20, saving $80 of their income. Clearly, we must import $40 of food from J-Land to keep our consumption of food at $100.''

''So,'' said Adam, ''in that first year we would run a trade deficit of $40, and J-Land would run a trade surplus of $40.''

''But,'' said Eve, ''let's now consider each future year. Both economies produce $120 of food, but we consume $100, and the J's consume $140. Clearly, we must export $20 of food to J-Land. So in each future year, we would run a trade surplus of $20, and J-Land would run a trade deficit of $20. Yet they would have the higher standard of living.''

''But the trade balance leaves out something important,'' exclaimed Adam. ''It includes only payments from the flow of goods—$20 of food. But while we're receiving $20 from the J's for food, we're paying $20 to the J's for interest on the original $40 loan.''

"Adam, that's impressive reasoning," smiled Eve. "You're right. We do need a balance that includes interest payments as well as payments for goods. I propose we call it the 'current account' balance. In each future year, our current account balance would be zero, because our receipts from $20 of food would be offset by our $20 of interest payments."

"But," sighed Adam, "even though our current account balance would be zero, and our trade balance would be a surplus of $20, our standard of living would be lower than J-Land's."

"Exactly right," smiled Eve.

"So," said Adam, "it would be a mistake for us to feel good about our current account balance of zero and our trade surplus of $20. Because what really matters is that the J's would be enjoying a higher standard of living since they had saved and accumulated more wealth. So even if the headlines focus on the trade and current account balances, the most important thing to watch is who is saving more and accumulating more wealth, because that's what clearly tells who will enjoy the higher standard of living in the future."

"Adam," said Eve with obvious affection and tears in her eyes, "you've made me truly happy. And now that we know the consequences of failing to save as much as the J's, my love, do we have the resolve to match the J's?"

Adam stood and looked at the horizon, where he could see the snowy peak of Mount Fuji faintly in the distance.

"I pledge to you, Eve, that we will save enough to finance not one, but two tractors. We will match the J's in wealth accumulation. Our children's standard of living will be second to none in the world."

And together, Adam and Eve walked bravely toward the sunset.

The relative saving rate

I know what you're thinking. Things were pretty simple in those days. Two couples, two countries, one currency (fig leaves), no population growth. So what happens if things get more complicated?

To answer this question, economists have constructed a model. In order to isolate the impact of a difference in the saving rate, the model assumes that our economy and the economy of the rest of the world are identical except that saving rates differ. There's no point keeping you in suspense. Here's what the model tells us. (The model is described in the technical appendix to this chapter.) If our saving rate exceeds the rest of the world's, then we will eventually achieve higher wealth, income, and consumption per person than the rest of the world. We will be a creditor nation and receive net interest payments from the rest of the world. We will consume more by being a net importer of goods, running a trade (in goods) deficit. But our current account will be in surplus, because our net interest earnings will exceed our trade deficit.

Conversely, if our saving rate is less than that of the rest of the world, then we will eventually suffer lower wealth, income, and consumption per person than the rest of the world. We will be a debtor nation and make net interest payments to the rest of the world. We will consume less by being a net exporter of goods, running a trade (in goods) surplus. But our current account will be in deficit, because our net interest payments will exceed our trade surplus. So according to economic analysis, our *relative* saving rate—how our saving rate compares with that of the rest of the world—is one key determinant of our current account and trade balances. And our major conclusion remains unchanged in an open economy with trade and capital flows: A permanent increase in our saving rate will eventually achieve higher consumption per person.

But does the economist's model capture all the complexity of the world economy? Of course not. Is the relative saving rate really the only determinant of a nation's relative standard of living and its current account and trade balances? Of course not. Don't things like natural resource endowments, real investment opportunities, and entrepreneurship matter? Certainly they do. And isn't an environment of private property rights and free markets important? Yes it is. Welcome to the real world. It's complicated.

But in a complicated world, we've got to simplify to make any progress. Not only that. We've got to concentrate on issues we can do something about. We can't change our basic natural resource endowment. But we can do something about our national saving rate. So that's where we focus our model, and our attention. And a simple message emerges: In an open economy, as well as a closed economy, a high relative saving rate is a key factor in obtaining a high relative standard of living.

The forest and the trees

You may have noticed that our analysis says nothing about particular products doing battle against foreign competitors in world markets. We present no box scores of your favorite products and industries. Why not? Because our task is to see the whole forest, not study particular trees. Of course, each company must work hard to hold its own against rivals, domestic or foreign. Each company should watch its own industry's box score and strive to increase its market share. But our task is different.

Looking at the forest, rather than particular trees, we have concluded that the key to winning the international standard of living competition is to make our saving rate higher than that of other nations. Does this mean that we don't care what our companies do? Should we tell our exporters to relax their efforts? Should we tell our import-competing firms to give up battling imports? Of course not. Whether our economy is open or closed, we should always exhort our producers to compete as vigorously as possible with domestic or foreign competitors, because such competitive effort leads to innovation and efficiency, and raises our standard of living.

But however excited we get about microeconomic competitions among particular companies in particular industries, we should not lose the macroeconomic perspective. Let each company worry about its particular tree. Our job is to worry about saving, because saving is the nourishment for the whole forest. It is the rich topsoil, the rainfall, the sunlight, the temperature. With plenty of saving, the forest will succeed. Of course, particular trees will struggle against each other. And the study of competition among particular trees is fascinating. But our job is to make sure that the forest as a whole does well, not that any particular tree succeeds.

In a world of international competition and trade, saving is a key factor. We should concentrate on achieving a high relative saving rate, thereby eventually accumulating more wealth per person than other nations. And that means concentrating on implementing the policies we have proposed for raising our national saving rate.

So who will emerge from the numerous international trade battles in countless industries with a standard of living that is second to none? Almost surely it will be the nation that sustains the highest saving rate decade after decade.

TECHNICAL APPENDIX
The Relative Saving Rate and Trade

I'm sure you want to know some of the assumptions behind our model.[1] Let me begin by telling you its simplifications. The model has two "countries"—our country and "the rest of the world" (every other country consolidated). Our country is small relative to the rest of the world, so that its behavior has little impact on the values of the rest of the world's economic variables. Except for scale, our country's economy and the "world's" economy are identical in every respect you can think of: they have the same population growth rate, the same production technology, and so on. And initially they have the same saving rate.

Now comes a key simplifying assumption: perfect capital mobility. This means that if savers discover they can earn a higher interest rate by lending abroad rather than at home, they shift their funds. This implies that capital will flow until the interest rate on domestic investment equals the interest rate on "world" investment.

But since the interest rate depends on the physical productivity of capital, and this in turn depends on capital per worker, it follows that our country and the rest of the world will always have the same capital per worker and hence, the same domestic output per worker. If our capital per worker stays the same as the rest of the world's as both labor forces grow, then our domestic physical investment per worker must be the same as the rest of the world's.

I'm sure you won't be surprised to learn that with everything identical, including the saving rate, these assumptions imply that our current account and trade balances are both zero, and that the United States is neither a creditor nor a debtor nation. It turns out that our domestic absorption—consumption plus investment—exactly equals our domestic output, so that any imports are exactly matched by exports, and our trade balance is zero.

Also, our country's domestic investment exactly matches our own saving, so any interest payments our savers earn from abroad are matched by interest payments from our firms to the world's savers; thus, *net* interest payments are zero. So our current account balance, which includes payments for goods and interest, is also zero. Our wealth is equal to our domestic capital stock. We own the same amount of the rest of the world's capital stock as the rest of the world owns of our capital stock. So we are neither a creditor nor debtor nation.

But now suppose our country permanently raises its saving rate, so that our saving rate exceeds the rest of the world's. What happens? The moment our saving rate rises, our consumption rate falls. So our domestic absorption—consumption plus investment—will immediately fall below our domestic output. Thus, the excess of output over absorption will be exported, and the immediate result will be a trade surplus. With net interest payments still zero, the result will also be a current account surplus equal to the trade surplus.

But net interest payments will not remain zero. Our saving now exceeds our domestic investment. Rather than confront diminishing returns at home, our excess saving will flow abroad to finance real investment in the world economy. But this means that our savers will earn net interest payments from abroad.

As our savers accumulate wealth—claims on the world capital stock—wealth per worker and income (including interest income) per worker will rise. But this means that consumption per worker will also rise, after its initial setback. It turns out that as long as the interest rate exceeds the labor force growth rate, consumption per worker will eventually surpass its initial level. When this happens, domestic absorption—consumption plus investment—will exceed domestic output, and the trade balance will reverse. We will become a net importer of goods.

In the final steady state, we will have a current account surplus, but a trade (in goods) deficit. The net interest payments our savers earn from the rest of the world will exceed the net payments we make to buy goods. We will also be a creditor nation, owning more of the rest of the world's capital stock than it owns of our capital stock.

Note that in the short run, after we raise our saving rate, we initially run a trade (in goods) surplus. The surplus gradually becomes a deficit only after we accumulate wealth, become a creditor nation, and earn enough interest from abroad to finance higher consumption per worker than the rest of the world.

Note

1. The model is presented in detail in Laurence Seidman "The Current Account and Trade Balances in a Neoclassical Growth Model" (University of Delaware Department of Economics Working Paper, July 1989), and is based on earlier work by Willem Buiter, "Time Preference and International Lending and Borrowing in an Overlapping-Generations Model," *Journal of Political Economy* 89 (August 1981), 769–97; and Philip Neher, *Economic Growth and Development: A Mathematical Introduction* (New York: John Wiley & Sons, 1971).

9

WHAT ABOUT POLLUTION AND DEPLETION?

How far we've come from the early 1970s. Remember Earth Day? Remember the homage we paid to the environment? Remember our alarm about finite natural resources? Here we are now at the dawn of the 1990s, and the author of this book is saying—or at least, seems to be saying—forget all that, let's rev up the engine of economic growth, and ride roughshod over the environment in a desperate attempt to avoid losing an international economic competition. Haven't we learned anything?

I hope we have learned something. Any book calling for faster economic growth has an obligation to respond to the concern about pollution and depletion. That is what this chapter is about.

A classic market failure

Let me give it to you straight. As an economist, I deny there is any problem. Whatever happens under the free market is automatically best, so pollution that occurs under a free market is "optimal," to use a favorite word among economists. Not only that. The GNP—our beloved gross national product—is all that really counts. Only soft-headed people care about things like the environment.

Is this your view of what the typical economist thinks about environmental pollution? I'll bet it is. Now I could succumb to a cheap temptation. I could say, "Yes, my narrow-minded colleagues think this way, but not I. I'm a more sensitive, broad-minded economist, who recognizes that the free market isn't perfect and that the GNP isn't everything." And if I did this, I might ingratiate myself, because you might think, "He's better than the typical narrow economist, who blindly worships the free market and the GNP."

I'm tempted. But I can't do it. Because I cannot live such a lie. Besides, my colleagues would never let me get away with it. Because the simple truth is this: All economists agree, and have agreed for many years, that the free market fails when it comes to environmental pollution. I am no better than my colleagues when I acknowledge, freely and without duress, that a free market generates too much pollution.

Not only that. I am no better than my colleagues when I acknowledge that the GNP is a very imperfect measure of economic well-being. In particular, all my colleagues agree that environmental quality and leisure are "goods" that are as valuable to people as the material goods that are counted in the GNP.

Now don't get me wrong. I am not going to claim that economists, as a group, are especially concerned about the environment. Some are, some aren't, like most any other group of citizens. But economists agree that if people value environmental quality, then we must judge the economy's performance by its provision of environmental quality as well as material goods. You may not associate humility with the economics profession. But most economists do pay homage—perhaps too much homage—to the humble doctrine of "consumer sovereignty." This requires a word of explanation.

In standard economics, economists humbly refuse to judge a consumer's preferences. If the typical consumer likes apples more than oranges, who are we to judge? We take consumer preferences as given, and then ask: How well does the economy satisfy these preferences?

How do economists, having become accustomed to humility,

respond when we discover that the typical consumer likes leisure and environmental quality, as well as apples, oranges, and other material goods? Naturally, we think, who are we to judge? So we give the preference for environmental quality and leisure the same respect as the preference for material goods.

Then, unanimously, we give the free market a failing grade for the poor environmental quality it generates. Even the most ardent free marketeer economists give it a failing grade in this department. But then we go a step further. We locate the source of the "market failure." The problem is that no one owns the air and water. There is a failure of property rights. May I explain?

Whenever something is "free," it is used wastefully. But anything that is owned is seldom free. Naturally, the owner insists on charging a price for its use, so any potential user is deterred from frivolous use. But who owns the air above City X, or the water in River Y? No one owns it, so no one charges a price for "using it"—that is, polluting it. Is it any wonder, then, that it is polluted excessively under a free market?

For virtually all economists, including me, the solution is straightforward. The government must step in and assume ownership on behalf of the public, and then do what a typical private owner of a resource does: charge a price for its use. In other words, the market fails because a key element—ownership of a valuable resource—is absent. The solution is to restore the market by restoring the missing ingredient: ownership of the resource, and a price for its use.

There are two ways in which the government can charge a price. By permit, and by tax. Under the permit method, the government decides the aggregate quantity of pollutant X it is willing to tolerate in a particular geographic region. It then auctions a quantity of permits to polluters, where each permit allows the owner to emit a specified amount of the pollutant. Emission of the pollutant without such a permit would be illegal. The permit price would be set by supply and demand. Under the tax method, the government sets a price—or tax—per unit of pollutant X in a particular geographic region. Polluters are then free to respond to this tax per unit of pollutant X.

Note the difference between the two methods. Under the permit method, the government fixes the aggregate quantity of pollutant X, but the bidding of polluters determines the price of a permit—hence, the price per unit of pollutant X. Under the tax method, the government fixes the price per unit of pollutant X, but the response of polluters determines the aggregate quantity of pollution.

Which method is better? It depends. We'll return to this question shortly. But note an important feature that the methods have in common. Under both methods, all polluters of pollutant X in a particular region face the same price per unit.

Facing the trade-off

Now imagine a violently lethal pollutant. Even the slightest bit of it would cause enormous casualties. What do economists say about that? The same thing as any other sensible citizen. Ban it. But we economists insist on viewing this as an extreme case of our two pricing methods. Under the permit method, the more harmful the pollutant, the smaller the aggregate number of permits that should be auctioned; in the extreme, the number auctioned should be zero. Under the tax method, the more harmful the pollutant, the higher the tax per unit of pollutant; in the extreme, the tax should be so high that no polluter can afford to emit even a single unit of it.

So economists have no problem with an extreme case. But we insist that society face up to the basic trade-off. At any moment, society has limited resources—labor, capital, land, and raw materials. If there were just two goods that could be produced, A and B, then more of A would imply less of B. The same is true if the two goods are environmental quality and material output. More of the first implies less of the second.

Suppose we want to force pollution to zero, thereby maximizing environmental quality. The less we pollute, the more material output we sacrifice. The sacrifice can take several forms. Polluters can simply cut back their products, and resources are then shifted to products people value less. Or polluters can switch to more costly production techniques that entail less pollution. The additional cost implies that more resources are absorbed, and fewer are available for other material output. Polluters, or government, can clean up pollution using resources that could have been used to make material output. However pollution is reduced, the result is a reduction in the total value of material output.

All that economists ask is that people face up to the trade-off. Consider again a violently lethal pollutant. Here's what economists would advise. Imagine allowing a single unit to be emitted. Estimate the harm done. Then estimate the additional material output that the emission would make possible. Compare the two. If you decide that the harm outweighs the benefit from the material output, then by all means ban the pollutant.

But now consider a less harmful pollutant. Suppose that emitting a single unit would not do much damage, but would allow a highly valued increase in material output. If the public decides that the harm from the extra pollution is less than the benefit from the extra output, then by all means allow this unit to be emitted. And now make the same comparison for a second unit. If the harm is still less than the benefit, then make the same comparison about a third unit.

As the amount of pollution rises, the harm from another unit of pollution is likely to rise, and the benefit from the associated output is likely to fall. So at some point, the harm from another unit will at last exceed the benefit. Clearly, pollution should be allowed up to this point, and no further. So at last we have arrived at the socially optimal amount of pollutant X. We've properly balanced the benefit from each unit of pollutant X against its harm or cost.

It's now safe to tell you something. You've just gone through an exercise in "marginal analysis"—the most fundamental technique in microeconomics. "Marginal analysis" means finding an optimum by reasoning one unit at a time. Did it seem simple, commonsensical? Don't be alarmed, but you may be an instinctive economist.

I hope you're thinking, "It sounds nice in theory, but isn't it hard to do in practice?" Absolutely. But it would be a great step forward if people realized that there is such a thing as a socially optimal amount of each pollutant, that except in an extreme case it is greater than zero, and that in theory we can locate it by marginal analysis—reasoning one unit at time.

Now to some practical problems. Air or water quality is a "public good." This means that it is impossible to improve the quality for me without also improving it for my neighbor. Yet I may care, and he may not. The same is true of national defense, another public good, but not true of a TV, which is a typical private good. I can easily get a higher quality TV while my neighbor sticks with his little black and white. But not so for environmental quality, or national defense.

Imagine that the government conducts a survey. An interviewer asks each citizen: "Be honest, how much would you pay to raise air quality from grade F to grade D?" Then the government sums the amount all honest citizens would be willing to pay, and compares it to the cost—the lost material output. If the sum of payments exceeds the cost of lost output, air quality should be increased to grade D. And then the government asks the same question about raising it from grade D to grade C. Once the sum of what people are willing to pay no longer exceeds the cost of another unit of quality, the government has arrived at the socially optimal grade of quality.

But there's a little practical problem. How can the government get citizens to be honest? After all, what would you think if a government interviewer came to your door and asked, "How much are you willing to pay for Z?" You might think, "If I tell him I'd be willing to pay $100 for Z, that's actually what he'll force me to pay." I'm sure you would be honest, but I'll bet you know someone who would understate his true willingness to pay.

Economists have tried to invent ingenious techniques to induce citizens to answer honestly. But although some progress has been made, such techniques are not often used. So we must admit that determining the socially optimal amount of pollutant X will be as imperfect, in practice, as determining the optimal amount of national defense, or police protection. Imperfectly, the legislature must simply do the best it can to weigh cost against benefit.

Why economists advocate pollution prices

What's so great about using prices for pollution? I have just admitted that locating the socially optimal quantity of any pollutant X is very difficult in practice. Once the target for pollutant X in a particular region is set, why not just assign a quota (ceiling) to each polluter of X, to assure that the aggregate quantity of X equals our target?

Now we come to the heart of the matter. Once the aggregate target has been set, how do we decide which firms should do the polluting—that is, how do we "allocate" pollution among the polluters? For example, suppose our aggregate target for pollutant X in region R is one thousand units, and there are one hundred polluters in the region. Perhaps the most natural approach would be for the government to mandate specific low-polluting production techniques for the polluters of X. In fact, this "technology-forcing" approach is generally taken by the U.S. government. Unfortunately, in this case it would be a poor way to handle the allocation problem. Why?

First of all, the hundred polluters of X produce a variety of products. Consumers value some of these products more than others. Surely we want the allocation to take account of consumer preference for the products. Second, the polluters differ in technological options. Some can cut back pollution easily with little additional cost. Others must incur a substantial cost increase to achieve the same reduction. Since polluters will pass on cost increases to consumers, we want the allocation to take account of these technological options.

It might seem that government agents could interview consumers about their preferences for products, and the polluters about their technological options. But these interviews would be costly, and of dubious value. It's far from obvious what questions to ask consumers. And while the questions are clearer for the polluters, why should they tell the truth? Wouldn't any polluter try to exaggerate the cost of cutback in order to win a higher ceiling?

I'm sure you've realized by now that interviews could also be used to decide how much to produce of any product, pollution aside. Fortunately, we don't use them. Instead, our price system gets the job done. Both consumers and producers respond to prices, and there is no need for government interviewers.

Let's see how pollution prices would handle the allocation problem. Consider the permit method. The government would auction off a thousand permits. Potential polluters of X would bid for the permits. The permit price—hence, the price per unit of pollutant X—would rise until the demand for permits by polluters was cut down to a thousand, equal to the available supply.

As the bidding begins, and the price is still zero, polluters want to pollute far more than a thousand units. But this causes the price to begin to rise. As the price rises, polluters reevaluate. Consider the polluter whose products have substitutes, so that consumers can easily shift away if the price rises much. This polluter will reason: "I can't afford to buy permits even at this low price, because when I try to pass the cost on to my customers, they will simply shift to substitutes." So this polluter drops out of the bidding.

By contrast, consider the polluter whose products have no substitutes, and are highly valued by consumers. This polluter will reason: "I can afford to buy permits even at this high price, because when I try to pass the cost on to my customers, I will succeed." So who ends up with few or no permits, and cuts pollution sharply? The polluter whose product has substitutes. And who ends up with a lot of permits, and cuts pollution relatively little? The polluter whose product has no substitutes and is highly valued by consumers. And this is exactly the pattern of cutback we want.

Next, consider the polluter with technological options that

enable a reduction in pollution at little additional cost. As the permit price rises, he reasons: "Rather than pay the permit price, it is cheaper for me to switch technologies and reduce pollution."

By contrast, consider the polluter with few technological options. Only at high cost can he reduce pollution. As the permit price rises, he reasons: "I'm still better off paying the permit price, because it would be even more expensive for me to switch technologies." So who ends up with few or no permits, and cuts back pollution sharply? The polluter with good technological options. And who ends up with many permits, and cuts back pollution relatively little? The polluter with few technological options. And this is exactly the pattern of reduction we want.

Suppose the permit price ends up $20 per unit of pollution. Then a $20 per unit pollution *tax* would produce exactly the same pattern of pollution reduction across polluters. After all, a polluter doesn't care whether the $20 per unit is called a permit price or a tax. He will figure his profit, and do the same thing. Therefore, whether the price is charged through the permit or tax method, the desirable pattern of cutback across polluters is induced. So we can see how a price system results in the socially optimal allocation of pollutant X across polluters. Is some more general principle at work here? Of course. A price system results in the socially optimal allocation of any resource across users—whether the resource is labor, capital, materials, or pollutant. One requirement of being an economist, since Adam Smith, is to understand this point. And that is why economists want to use prices to allocate pollution among polluters.

There is another way to put this. We can fight over what the target for pollutant X should be. Should it be eight hundred units, or twelve hundred units, instead of one thousand units? I have already admitted that it is tough to answer this question in practice, and economists don't claim to offer any good way of selecting the target. But once the target has been set, we can surely agree on this: let's achieve the pollution target with the minimum sacrifice in material output.

That is exactly what pollution prices can do. Pollution prices induce a socially desirable pattern of pollution reduction across polluters. This means that the target is achieved with the minimum loss in the value of material output. You might (or might not, admittedly) be interested to learn that this point can be proved mathematically.

The passionate objector

But alas, a passionate objector has risen to his feet and will keep silent no longer. He cries, "Isn't a pollution price a 'license to pollute' and therefore reprehensible?" I'm afraid, my passionate friend, that you've confused two distinct tasks: first, what should be the aggregate target; and second, given the target, how should we allocate the pollution among polluters? Prices only apply to the second task, while you are really concerned about the first task—the setting of the target. No doubt, you want a target of zero. Fine, make your case, and we will listen. If you succeed, then we will simply ban the pollutant. But if you fail to convince us, and we decide to tolerate a certain amount of pollutant X, then surely even you will agree that we should achieve the target with the minimum sacrifice in material output. And that's where prices come in.

Our passionate objector shifts his ground, and asks, "Won't the polluters just pass on these pollution prices to me, an innocent consumer, by raising product prices to cover these charges?" Yes, answers any honest economist, they certainly will. "And," continues our righteous objector, "why should I pay for their foul pollution? Let them pay for it!"

I'm afraid, my passionate objector, that once again you have missed the point. The whole object of pollution prices is to confront consumers with the environmental cost of the products they buy. The price system is an information system. The price of each product is supposed to convey information to the consumer—namely, the cost of producing it. If the price is less than cost, then the consumer is misled, and demands too much of the good; if the price is greater than cost, then the consumer demands too little of the good. The free market fails because the price of high-polluting (HP) output is too low relative to the price of low-polluting (LP) output. Why is the price of HP output too low? Because it does not include the environmental cost. And why not? For the simple reason that polluters are not charged for polluting. And why aren't they charged? Because there is no owner of air or water to impose the charge. So consumers are induced, by the false price signals, to consume too much HP output and too little LP output. The whole point of pollution prices is to raise the price of HP output relative to the price of LP output, so that consumers receive accurate information, and as a result shift consumption from HP to LP products.

"But is this fair?" replies our objector. "Is it fair that I, an innocent consumer, should pay, instead of the dirty polluters?"

I beg your pardon, but what do you mean, innocent? You are enjoying a product that entails pollution. Yes, the producer did the dirty work, and now you want to enjoy the product without any responsibility for what its production required. How admirable!

Also, to whom do you want to shift the burden? The inanimate corporation? Alas, there is a little obstacle to your strategy, and it is this: Business firms don't bear burdens, only people do. The people may be consumers, workers, stockholders, or managers. But it is ostrichlike to hope that lifeless corporations, not flesh-and-blood people, will bear the burden. So the debate is really about which people should bear it.

Most economists take this position: Let each consumer pay a price that reflects the cost of the product so that the price system conveys accurate information, and each person pays the cost of whatever he consumes. Then pursue fairness by adjusting the degree of progressivity of the personal tax—whether income or consumption—as discussed in chapters 3 and 6. Distorting the information value of the price system is a poor way to pursue fairness.

Somewhat subdued, our objector at last asks a better question.

"But aren't there some practical problems with your two pricing methods that you've been concealing?"

Well, concealing isn't the right word. But I'll admit I haven't gotten around to them. So let's consider a few problems. Perhaps the most important practical obstacle is this: pricing requires metering—measuring each polluter's emissions—while mandating low-polluting technologies does not. In some cases, metering may be too costly or unfeasible. Naturally, economists recommend using pricing only if the cost of metering is less than the benefit of pricing.

The tax method can never guarantee that the pollution target will be achieved. In response to a given tax per unit, polluters may emit too much, or too little. If too much, the government can raise the tax; if too little, the government can lower it. But the government may never hit it just right, and it is possible that it will keep missing by a wide margin.

Of course, we should keep this problem in perspective. Earlier, we saw that selecting the target is extremely difficult in the first place. No selected target should be regarded as sacrosanct, because it surely differs from the social optimum. So moderately missing the target should not be viewed with alarm, because the target itself is probably not the social optimum.

The permit method seems to guarantee that the target will be achieved because the government auctions off only the target number of permits. But the permit method has its problems. Will the auction occur on a single day for the year? What if a firm decides it needs more or fewer permits as the year progresses? Will the permits be transferable? Will there be a continuous market for permits? Who will be allowed to bid for permits? And so forth.

The permit method may be less practical than the tax method. For a hundred firms, it may be feasible. For millions of motorists, it clearly is not. So in many applications, the price will have to be a tax, and there will be no guarantee that aggregate pollution will achieve the target.

Nothing is perfect in practice, of course. But the price system has worked well in practice, not simply in theory, for our economy as a whole. Few doubt that economies guided by prices perform much more efficiently than economies that try to operate without prices. So it makes sense to use prices for environmental pollution.

Thus far, neither the United States nor any other nation has relied heavily on pollution prices to implement environmental policy. Should economists surrender to despair? Not at all. The cause of pollution prices has slowly begun to make progress. Some recent experiments with pollution prices (in the form of transferable emission permits) give grounds for hope. Nevertheless, we must confess that governments still generally mandate specific production techniques for polluters. So we continue to achieve a given level of environmental quality with an unnecessarily large sacrifice in material output.

Faster growth and pollution

Will faster growth doom us to more pollution? Not necessarily. Suppose that today, one hundred units of output are accompanied by ten units of pollution. Isn't it inevitable that two hundred units of output will be accompanied by twenty units of pollution? Not necessarily. The key to breaking the link between output and pollution is substitution: of low-polluting goods for high-polluting goods, and of low-polluting production technology for high-polluting production technology.

Material output consists of many goods and services. With today's technology, some are high-polluting (HP) and others are low-polluting (LP). Even if technology remained the same, we could raise our total output without raising pollution if we shifted the composition of our output from HP to LP goods.

How can we induce such a shift? I'm sure you can guess. By gradually raising our set of pollution prices as our output grows. This will raise the price of HP goods relative to the price of LP goods, and consumers will be induced to shift their demand from HP to LP goods. Producers will therefore be compelled to shift production from HP to LP goods.

Moreover, production technology can be shifted as output grows. Many goods can be produced using alternative methods that generate different amounts of pollution. We could raise our total output, without increasing pollution, by shifting from high- to low-polluting production technologies, using pollution prices as a deterrent against the use of HP technology. Such prices would make it profitable for firms to reduce the pollution that accompanies output by shifting to low-polluting production technologies.

So can we grow faster without reducing environmental quality? Yes. But to do so, we must gradually raise our set of pollution prices as our output grows, thereby inducing these substitutions as growth takes place.

It is true that, as output grows, it gets "harder" to maintain a given level of environmental quality in this sense: if nothing were done to change the mix of HP and LP goods, or the mix of HP and LP production technologies, then environmental quality would deteriorate. All the more reason for using pollution prices (through auctioned permits or taxes), rather than mandated production techniques, to implement environmental policy. The more importance we attach to raising output per person, the more important it is to maintain environmental quality with the minimum sacrifice in material output.

Faster growth and depletion

Watch how this section repeats the same argument as the last section. To make sure you grasp the similarity, I will even use many of the same phrases.

Will faster growth be stalled by resource depletion? Again, not necessarily. Suppose that today, one hundred units of output is accompanied by the depletion of ten units of a natural resource. Isn't it inevitable that two hundred units of output will be accompanied by depletion of twenty units of the natural resource? Fortunately, not necessarily.

Would it surprise you to learn that the key to breaking the link between output and natural resources is substitution: of goods whose production requires low amounts of natural resources (LR goods) for goods whose production requires high amounts of natural resources (HR goods), and of LR production technologies for HR production technologies?

Material output consists of many goods and services. With today's technology, some are "high-resource-using" (HR), and others are "low-resource-using" (LR). Even if technology stayed the same, we could raise our total output, without raising depletion, if we shifted the composition of our output from HR to LR goods.

How can such a shift be induced? I'm sure you can guess: by a rise in natural resource prices. If this happens, the price of HR goods will rise relative to the price of LR goods, consumers will be induced to shift demand from HR to LR goods, and producers will therefore be compelled to shift production from HR to LR goods.

Moreover, production technology can be shifted as output grows. Many goods can be produced with alternative technologies that utilize different amounts of natural resources. We could raise our total output, without raising depletion, by shifting from high to low-resource-using production technologies.

How can such a shift be induced? I'm absolutely sure you can guess: by a rise in natural resource prices. If this happens, it will be profitable for firms to reduce the depletion that accompanies output by shifting to low-resource-using production technologies.

But now we come to an important difference between pollution and depletion. The government sets pollution prices, so it is up to the government to raise them as output grows. But it is the market that sets natural resource prices. So the key question becomes: Will the market raise resource prices as output grows?

The best way to know the answer is to imagine, pleasantly, that you are a resource owner. Your resource lies underground, and you have the option of mining it and selling it to firms for production today, or holding it in the ground to await a future price. What do you do? How much do you mine and sell, and how much do you keep underground?

Suppose you read that scientists are on the verge of a breakthrough that will provide a cheap, abundant substitute for your resource. As a citizen, you are overjoyed at the advance of mankind through brainpower. As a resource owner, you are desperate. There is no point holding your resource underground to await a future price. So you mine and sell at full capacity.

Now instead, suppose you read that scientists regard such a breakthrough as unlikely, so your resource, growing scarcer each year, will command a rising price in future years. As a citizen, you are in despair over the failure of brainpower to advance mankind. As a resource owner, you can hardly conceal your glee. Why sell to the market today when a much higher price awaits you in the future? Even if you need cash, it would be better to borrow than to foolishly mine and sell at full capacity. So you hold most of your resource underground, as do other owners of your resource. Its price rises immediately, inducing firms to cut down on current utilization.

But look what has happened. Lo and behold, conservation has been achieved. You and your fellow resource owners have cut down mining and selling, and kept most of your resource underground. Of course, your motive was not exactly noble. In fact, the word "conservation," with its public-spirited connotation, never entered your mind. In truth, the word "profit," not "conservation," was on your smiling lips as you fell asleep each night.

But old Adam Smith would not have been surprised. In your pursuit of profit, you advanced the public welfare. With the threat of your resource becoming scarce in the future, the market gave you a profit signal to conserve now. And so you did. Immediately, your cutback in mining and selling raised your resource's price, and induced a cutback in its utilization. We did not have to rely on your benevolence, but only your self-interest, to slow the depletion of your resource. So without any government action, the market will automatically tend to generate the desired rise in resource prices as output grows.

We haven't even mentioned another important consequence of the rise in current prices and anticipated future prices. You and your fellow miners will go exploring. With high prices, more exploration is worth it. Also, scientists will go to work trying to invent substitutes. With high prices, there's a lot of money to be saved in finding alternatives. So not only do high prices cut current use, they also create incentives for long-term solutions.

Can it really be this simple? Unfortunately, no. The market can make mistakes. After all, no one has a crystal ball. Everyone may underestimate the difficulty of finding substitutes for your resource. So everyone may underestimate the future price of your resource. You and other owners may decide to mine and sell too much today. In the future, everyone may regret it.

So it would be naive to believe that the market handles the depletion problem perfectly. But it should be some consolation that the market has the tendency to conserve any resource that threatens to grow scarce in the future, and to induce the invention of substitutes.

Substituting capital for resources

Suppose we believe that some important resources will grow scarce in the future. Should we save more, or less? Should we accumulate more capital—physical, human, and knowledge—or less? A moment's reflection should tell us that our best chance to stave off a future decline in our standard of living is to save more, and accumulate more capital that can substitute for the depleting resources.

The production of output depends on labor, capital, and natural resources. If labor grows scarce, more capital can make up for it. Similarly, if natural resources grow scarce, then once again, our best chance for preserving output is to have more capital to make up for it.

Probably the most important capital to accumulate is knowledge capital: the blueprints of how to make new products, and how to make the same products differently. If we see resources vanishing, we need to cut our consumption and devote more of our labor force to investment in knowledge capital in order to invent ways around the coming depletion.

So capital accumulation and conservation are allies, not enemies. If a resource is being depleted, there are two things we can do to try to protect our future: we can conserve by cutting down on current utilization of the resource; and we can accumulate more capital—especially knowledge capital—so that we are able to get by with less of the resource in the future. Concern about resource depletion is no reason to cut saving and capital accumulation. On the contrary, it is an important reason to save more and accumulate capital faster.

Does it surprise you that conservation and capital accumulation are allies? It shouldn't. Both are ways of protecting the future standard of living, and both require sacrifices in current consumption. Those who care little about the future will deplete and consume. But those who want to protect the future will conserve and save.

10

EDUCATION, CHOICE, AND COMPETITION

The extraterrestrial visitor seemed delighted by the mechanism called competition.

"My discoveries on earth have been simply fascinating," XT exclaimed to his American host in remarkable English. "But perhaps more than anything else, this mechanism you use to improve productive performance is absolutely astonishing. After all, who would have thought it would work best?"

His host seemed puzzled. "I don't understand," he asked. "Isn't it obvious that competition is the best way to achieve better goods and services?"

"Not at all," replied XT. "You think it is obvious because you are so used to it. But it's not obvious at all. Where I come from, everyone would be simply amazed. They would say that the best way to do something is to create a single enterprise. Let the best minds come together in the enterprise, and plot its course. Then let everyone cooperate and get the job done. And by all means, don't let other enterprises proliferate, and wastefully duplicate effort. One cooperative effort, working in harmony for a single goal, is surely better than many enterprises working at cross-purposes, engaged in petty rivalry with each other."

"But," said XT's American host, "in the United States we call such a single enterprise a 'monopoly.' It's not a nice word in my country. A monopoly feels little pressure to perform well, because it has a captive audience. Consumers must buy its product. They have nowhere else to turn, no matter how poor a job the monopoly does. And the monopoly knows it. So the monopoly slacks off. It retains unproductive workers. It innovates slowly. And it responds sluggishly to consumer complaints.''

"I know, I know," exclaimed XT. "What a contrast between your economic system and the Soviet one. I'll never forget the long line at the Moscow department store. The poor Russians! How they grumbled. And how naive I was. I thought, they must be willing to wait this long because the products are so wonderful. When I finally reached the front of the line, I couldn't believe it. What shoddy merchandise. But the poor devils simply had no choice.''

"But XT," said his host, "you should have expected it. The Soviet economy consists of monopolies. Oh sure, they are public monopolies, run by the state, supposedly dedicated to serving the people. But a monopoly is a monopoly. Whether it's public or private hardly matters. When consumers have no choice, when producers feel no pressure from competition, the result is the same: poor performance, shoddy goods and services.''

"How astonishing," exclaimed XT, "but you are right. I have seen it with my own eyes. It's not even close. Competition dramatically outperforms monopoly every time. You should be quite proud of your little mechanism called competition.''

"We are," beamed his American host, "we are.''

XT's confusion

"But," continued XT, "there is something that confuses me. I hope you won't take offense at the questions I am about to ask.''

"Not at all," replied his host with confidence. "Fire away.''

"Well," said XT slowly, "you have been telling me how important capital accumulation is for advancing the standard of living, and how capital consists of human and knowledge, as well as physical capital. Am I correct?''

"Absolutely," replied the host.

"Now," continued XT, "schools are an important producer of human capital—of education—are they not?"

"Of course."

"And isn't it important to get the best possible performance from these producers of education?"

"Naturally," replied the host.

"In fact," continued XT, "wouldn't you agree that it is more important to get excellent performance from producers of education than from producers of say, furniture or appliances?"

"I certainly would agree," replied his host.

"So," asked XT cautiously, "please don't take offense, but why do you use local monopolies to produce education?"

The host felt struck by a bolt from the blue. He simply hadn't seen it coming. For a moment he was speechless.

"After all," continued XT, "you are engaged in an intense international competition over the future standard of living. Human capital—education—is going to be a key determinant of how you do in that competition. I would have thought that here would be the most important place to use your astonishing mechanism of competition to get the best performance possible. And to my surprise, I find this is one of the few areas where you tolerate monopoly. I'm afraid I don't understand."

"But," sputtered his host, at last able to speak, "we simply don't believe in competition for education. It's just not right."

"I still don't understand," said XT.

"Well, when it comes to education, we believe that each community should form a single enterprise, called a public school. We believe that the best minds in each community should come together in this enterprise and plot its course. Then everyone should cooperate and get the job done. And by all means, we shouldn't let other enterprises proliferate, and wastefully duplicate effort. One cooperative effort, working in harmony for a single goal, is surely better than many enterprises working at cross-purposes, engaged in petty rivalry with each other."

"Why," exclaimed XT, "that's the way everyone on my planet

thinks. Are you sure you haven't visited there? That's what I thought until I came to earth and discovered your marvelous invention, competition.''

"But education is different," said his host.

"Yes," said XT, "it's more important. All the more reason to use your best weapon, competition. Please forgive me if I quote you. Didn't you tell me earlier that a monopoly feels little pressure to perform well because it has a captive audience? Consumers must buy its product. They have nowhere else to turn no matter how poor a job it does. So the monopoly slacks off. It retains unproductive workers. It innovates slowly. And it responds sluggishly to consumer complaints. Did I dream it, or weren't these your very words?"

"Yes, yes, they were," muttered his host. "But our local monopolies are dedicated to serving the community."

"Yes," replied XT, "but didn't you also say that a monopoly is a monopoly? Whether it's public or private hardly matters. When consumers have no choice, when producers feel no pressure from competition, the result is the same: poor performance, shoddy goods and services."

"Maybe I did say that," admitted the host reluctantly. "But our local monopolies are different. Our teachers and principals are very dedicated. And the consumers—parents—form associations that monitor the school. They do apply pressure. And there is also pressure from parents through the election of school board members."

"I am sure that most of your teachers and principals are dedicated," replied XT. "I am sure your parent associations and school board elections do apply some pressure. But it is curious, you will admit, that where it counts most—education—you have decided to use monopoly instead of competition."

"I never even realized we had a choice," admitted the host.

A variable voucher plan

"Would you indulge me?" XT asked his host. "I have been so

taken with your little mechanism of competition that I just can't help trying to figure out how it might be used in education. Maybe you're right. Maybe public monopoly is better in education. But do you mind if I give it a try?''

"No, go right ahead," replied his host. "But I'm sure you'll find it futile."

"Good," said XT. "Now I may make some false starts. But whenever you object, I will try to correct my plan to handle your objection. May I begin?"

"By all means."

XT began. "Why not simply end taxation for schools, and let parents use their own money to buy education for their children? I'm sure private schools would spring up. Each community would probably retain its public school, but now the school would have to raise its revenue by charging a price—tuition—just like the private schools. So private and public schools would compete, and parents would choose."

The host smiled. "I can't blame you for making this mistake, because on your planet, each household has roughly the same income. So each has the same ability to buy things. But perhaps you haven't noticed, in your fascination with our competition, that here on earth households differ greatly in income, and hence, in ability to buy things. So under your proposal, the rich would buy more education than the middle class, and the poor might not be able to buy any education at all."

"I see," said XT thoughtfully. "And this would be very unfair, I agree. Because a child's opportunity, through education, shouldn't depend on his parents' income."

"Exactly," smiled the host. "So I'm afraid we don't need to go any further. Competition in education would simply be unfair."

"Please, please," pleaded XT, "indulge me. On my planet, we like to solve problems, and we don't give up so easily. Let me see what I can do about your important objection."

After a long pause, XT spoke. "How about this. Once again, end local school taxes, so the public school must charge tuition, just like private schools. But let the state government raise taxes, and then use the revenue to reimburse each household a fixed sum per child. You might call the sum a 'voucher.' The voucher would assure that even the poor could afford a decent education."[1]

"Your proposal is better," admitted the host, "but it's still not good enough. While it would guarantee the poor a minimum, education would still vary greatly with income. The rich would add a lot to their vouchers and buy a lot of education, the middle class would add a little, and the poor would add nothing at all. So there would still be great inequality."

"True," said XT. "But why not prohibit 'add-ons'? Everyone would have to spend the same amount on education—the voucher amount."

"I'm surprised at you," said the host. "I thought you wanted to give consumers—parents—a choice. And while they may be free to choose among schools, they would have no freedom whatsoever to spend more on education if you prohibited 'add-ons.' Besides, does it make sense to let people spend as much as they want on all kinds of things, but rigidly limit what they can spend on education?"

"You're right," admitted XT. "Prohibiting 'add-ons' is too rigid. I don't want rigid uniformity, and I don't want to limit a household's spending on education."

"So what do you want?" asked the host.

"I want to move toward *income neutrality*," replied XT. "I want households with the same desire for education to be able to spend roughly the same amount per child regardless of income. But I don't want a straitjacket. I want a household, rich or poor, that gives a high priority to education, to be able to spend more than the guaranteed minimum. How can I achieve this flexibility?"

XT thought for some time. Then he exclaimed, "I've got it. Why not make the voucher *variable*? Why not let it vary according to a household's income and education spending? Here's how it would work.[2]

"Any household that spends exactly the guaranteed minimum would receive a voucher that covers 100 percent of its expense.

But if a household spent more than the minimum, its voucher would increase. The increase would be greater for a low-income household than for a high-income household.''

"I don't understand," said the host. "Could you give me an example?''

"Certainly," replied XT. "Suppose the state decides that the minimum guarantee should be $3,500 per child. Then any household that spends $3,500 would receive a $3,500 voucher—a 100 percent reimbursement from the state. But suppose the household spends $1,000 more—$4,500. If it is a low-income household, its voucher would increase by $800 to $4,300; if it is middle-income, its voucher would increase by $500 to $4,000; and if it is high-income, its voucher would increase by $200 to $3,700.

"So under the variable voucher," continued XT, "households would be free to buy more than the guaranteed minimum, but the tendency for the rich to spend more than the poor would be reduced.''

"But," asked the host, "would you really place all households in just three income groups? There would be a wide gap between the income levels at the top and bottom of each group.''

"No. I only used three groups to make my example simple. Actually, the voucher would vary smoothly with income. Take the middle-income group. While in my example, the average middle-income household would have its voucher raised $500 when it buys an additional $1,000 of education, the increment would be more than $500 for those below average, and less than $500 for those above average. The same for the low- and high-income groups.''

"Isn't this complicated?" asked the host.

"Not at all," replied XT. "The state government would include a voucher table in the state income tax booklet that would be mailed to every household.[3] The table would show the voucher for each income bracket (row) and education expenditure bracket (column). When the household records its annual income on its tax return, it would then know which income bracket row of the voucher table is relevant for the coming year. The row relevant to the household's income would show its voucher for different education expenditures. When the household considers a school, it can use the table to find its voucher, or reimbursement, should it decide to enroll.''

"I've got some practical questions about the mechanics," said the host. "Suppose I enroll my child at school S, which charges $4,500 tuition. What happens?"

"You get a bill for $4,500 from school S," replied XT. "Immediately, you mail your bill to the state tax agency which then determines your voucher according to your most recent state income tax return and the voucher table. It also makes sure your school is accredited, so that you are eligible for reimbursement. Then the state tax agency sends you a voucher check, made out to you, and returns your tuition bill. You deposit the voucher check at your bank, and mail the tuition bill to your school with a check for $4,500. By state law, the bank will only be permitted to deposit the voucher into your account when it receives, from the school, your check paying the tuition bill. So you will not be able to collect the state's voucher unless you pay your tuition bill.''

"Why not just have the state tax agency pay the school directly?" asked the host.

"Because," answered XT, "it is important to make it clear that the state government reimburses households, and has no direct financial link with schools. This will help insulate schools from government interference and regulation beyond the standard accreditation procedure. Also, notice that every parent, rich or poor, writes a check for the entire tuition bill to the school. The school doesn't know how much the parent is being reimbursed by the tax agency, so it never learns the parent's income.''

Choice and competition[4]

"So what would happen if your variable voucher plan were implemented?" asked the host.

"The most important thing that would happen," replied XT, "is that each public school would feel real competitive pressure.

For the first time, public school teachers and principals would be in the same situation as employees at any other firm in our economy. They would hear this simple message, loud and clear: Outperform other schools, and you will attract students and reap financial rewards; underperform other schools, and you will face an exodus of students and suffer the financial consequences.''

"But," asked the host, "aren't many of these teachers and principals dedicated individuals with fine motives?"

"Of course," said XT. "But so are many other people in many other firms and occupations in your economy. Yet the international evidence is undeniable. People produce better goods and services under the pressure of competition.''

"But aren't most teachers and principals working hard? How can competition make them do any better?"

"Competition doesn't simply make you work harder," replied XT. "It makes you work better and more intelligently. It forces you to constantly reevaluate whether you are using the best techniques. It doesn't let you continue a habit just because it's comfortable. It shakes things up.''

"But don't today's teachers and principals try to innovate and improve their techniques?" asked the host.

"Many do," answered XT. "But consider a school with mediocre performance. Without competition, it can go along indefinitely. With competition, its very existence may be in jeopardy. Which environment is likely to generate improvement?"

"It all sounds very nice in theory. But can you give me an example?" asked the host.

"Yes, I can," replied XT. "I actually observed this with my own eyes. My example concerns an inner city high school. In ninth grade, students coming from various junior high schools were placed in math and English classes without regard to their preparation. I visited an algebra class. A third of the students were well prepared for algebra, a third were barely prepared, and a third had never mastered the basics of arithmetic. The spread in preparation was enormous.''

"Why were they all in the same class?" asked the host.

"Apparently," replied XT, "because it was simpler for the schedulers, and it avoided the need to test entering students. When I asked teachers about it, no one defended the situation. In fact, most teachers complained about it. But they shrugged their shoulders, and told me that's just the way it is.

"At any rate, you can imagine what the class was like. The teacher had to decide what pace to set. But whatever pace she chose would only be best for a third of the students. The teacher I observed aimed at the middle group. Of course, the best prepared students were bored, and learned well below their capacity. And the least prepared students were still lost."

XT continued. "Don't make the mistake of thinking that at least the middle third received ideal treatment. The least prepared one-third were disruptive. How would you behave if you felt humiliated every day because you couldn't understand anything the teacher wrote on the board? And the best one-third joked around to relieve their boredom. So even the middle one-third learned well below their capacity, despite the fact that the teacher tried to aim at them."

"What was it like in the English classes?" asked the host.

"Just as bad," answered XT. "Students who could read above grade level were mixed with students who could hardly read at all. So what books could the teacher assign and discuss? No one seemed to have a good answer. Most teachers were very frustrated."

"But why was this situation allowed to continue?" asked the host.

"The answer is simple," replied XT. "There was no effective pressure on the school to make the extra effort to test entering students and devise a more complicated method of scheduling. Don't get me wrong. This was no cynical plot. The principal, teachers, and staff did not consciously say, 'Parents have to send their kids here, so we can slack off.' But there was simply no urgent pressure on the school. It would survive very nicely whether it remedied the situation or not.

"In fact," continued XT, "I asked the guidance office about it.

They would have had to administer the tests, and devise the more complicated class schedule. I asked them why they don't do this. Most teachers want it. They replied that they didn't have the resources, the personnel. I said, 'Why don't you try to get money from the board of education, or the superintendent of the public schools?' They said to me, 'How long have you been around here?'

"In a way," said XT, "I can't blame these guidance counselors. They knew that the burden of testing and scheduling would fall on them and add to their work load, and that they would receive little or no compensation for it. So naturally they resisted. And their resistance was successful because the school could survive forever without change. There was simply no crisis.

"Now, imagine what would have happened under the voucher plan. The most alert and informed parents would have jumped at the chance to switch their ninth-graders to schools that would place them in a class where the pace would be best for them."

"But what about the many parents who may not have realized what was going on?" asked the host.

"Other public schools or private schools would have recognized an untapped market. They would have carried the message to these parents. How? Many ways. They would have urged the alert, informed parents who had already enrolled their children to spread the word among neighbors and friends. They would have advertised in local media. They might even have employed some parents as recruiters. You can be sure that they would have found a way to get the message out, given the potential revenues at stake.

"Suddenly," continued XT, "this public school would have found itself in jeopardy, as parents removed their children. The school would have faced a financial crisis and a simple choice: either put students in classes suited to them, or watch the school go out of business, and lose your job. Then the guidance office would have been no match for the teachers and administrators alarmed about the school's survival and their own jobs."

"But is a voucher plan really necessary to get action? Couldn't the parents go to school meetings and complain?'' asked the host.

''Be realistic,'' replied XT. ''First, many parents are reluctant to try to argue with teachers and principals about education, even if they sense something is wrong. Second, without a voucher system, no other school has an incentive to inform them about problems in their school. Finally, and most important, the school doesn't need to listen to parents in order to stay in business and prosper.''

''I guess your plan is best for parents and children,'' admitted the host. ''But what about the teachers, principals, and guidance counselors? Is it fair to apply such pressure to them?''

''I don't see why not,'' replied XT. ''Millions of other Americans feel the same pressure. Do a good job, and the market rewards you. Do a poor job, and the market penalizes you. Why should they be exempt?''

''But,'' said the host, ''you must admit that your plan will hurt teachers and principals.''

''No, I won't admit it because it is not so,'' responded XT. ''True, poor teachers and principals will lose. But good teachers and principals will gain. Public and private schools will bid for the best teachers and principals. The board of each public school will recognize that unless it raises the compensation of these talented individuals, it will lose them, and parents will follow. So the best teachers and principals will be the beneficiaries of a bidding competition between public and private schools.''

''Are you saying,'' asked the host, ''that market competition will automatically generate 'merit pay' for teachers and principals?''

''Exactly,'' responded XT. ''Why is 'merit pay' an issue in the public, monopoly sector of the economy, but seldom discussed in the competitive private sector? Because the sheltered public sector monopoly can survive forever without merit pay, while competition automatically forces merit pay on many private firms.''

''So far you seem to be talking about how competitive pressure on schools will benefit the average student,'' said the host. ''But what about the student with special needs or problems?''

"Why, that is a particular strength of my plan," exclaimed XT. "Imagine a public school that does a good job for the majority of students. But for child P, the school isn't working. Parent P now can afford to seek another school. No longer is the parent trapped. And the school knows it. So the school will probably try to address the needs of the particular child. And if the parent is still not satisfied, the parent can switch."

"You know," admitted the host, "I should have realized that market competition would be better for consumers with special needs. Look at the difference between the Soviet economy and the American economy. The Soviet monopolies take the simplest approach. They make standardized goods aimed at the average consumer. They have no incentive to pay attention to the needs or desires of the 'nonaverage' consumer. But in the American economy, there is profit to be made by going after all kinds of consumers. Whenever a segment of consumers is unhappy with the standard product, producers can make profit by tailoring goods or services to their preferences. Somehow, I just never realized that the same process could be unleashed for education."

"And it is much more important to unleash it for education," added XT. "Yes, it's frustrating if parents can't get exactly the refrigerator they want. But this is nothing compared to the frustration of parents who can't get a school to address the special educational needs of their child. Can anyone doubt that market competition is more important in education than in refrigerators?"

Objections

"I like what you're saying," said the host. "But you will admit, won't you, that there are some potential problems with a variable voucher plan?"

"Of course there are," said XT. "But on my planet, we don't reject a plan just because it has some potential or even actual negatives. We try to figure out the best way to minimize the problems. Then we compare the pluses to the minuses of the plan.

If the pluses have the edge we still go with it. So may I make a proposal? Why don't you raise your objections, and I'll do the best I can to address them. Then, when we're all done, we can compare the pluses and minuses, and see if our conclusion is still 'go'."

"Fair enough," replied the host. "Let me start with a practical objection. How can schools possibly plan ahead under your voucher system? Today, school systems have enough trouble estimating enrollments and preparing for the students by hiring teachers and constructing facilities. With vouchers, planning will become impossible. And the casualties will be children. Unexpectedly, classes will be either too large or too small. And in some cases, children will find no school able to take them. We cannot afford chaos in something as vital as education."

"Is education more vital than food?" replied XT. "Do you ever worry at night about food?"

"What do you mean?" asked the host.

"Well, do you worry that the next time you need food, the stores won't have it?"

"No, that possibility has never even occurred to me," replied the host.

"You are aware," continued XT, "that your government makes no effort to assure that each community always has enough food in its stores. Food production, transportation, and distribution, are left to many competing firms, each seeking profit, with no central coordination. Doesn't that worry you?"

"Not in the least," replied the host.

"But your family would starve if this chaotic, competitive system failed your community for just a few days," said XT.

"But it never fails," said the host, "so I don't worry about it."

"So why should you worry about the planning task of competing schools?" asked XT. "After all, most students would remain year after year at the same school, and advance enrollment would give schools several months to make final adjustments, just as it does in the college system."

"But," responded the host, "how much simpler planning

would be if there were only a single school system.''

''That's what the Soviets say about every product,'' replied XT. ''When I visited the Soviet planners, they ridiculed your chaotic competition, and boasted how much easier it is to plan when there is a single producer. But look at the result. Your 'chaotic' competition generates high quality goods and services, and high levels of consumer satisfaction, while their unified planning generates shoddy goods and services, and widespread consumer dissatisfaction.''

''Let me turn to the problem of racial discrimination,'' said the host. ''What happens if a school refuses to accept black students, and because enough whites prefer such discriminatory schools, the discrimination is profitable?''

''Isn't that the same situation you used to have in many hotels, restaurants, movie theaters, and other public accommodations?'' asked XT.

''Exactly,'' replied the host.

''And didn't you pass the Civil Rights Act in 1964 making such racial discrimination illegal?''

''We did,'' answered the host.

''Well,'' asked XT, ''how has it worked out? Do these hotels, restaurants, movie theaters, and so on, still exclude blacks?''

''No, almost all of them accept blacks. Civil rights leaders seldom complain about discrimination in public accommodations any more.''

''Well,'' replied XT, ''clearly your Civil Right Act should cover schools. Racial discrimination in admission should be illegal.''

''But,'' continued the host, ''it's not so simple. Since the Civil Rights Act, a controversy has simmered in our nation over whether each business firm should be required to have sufficient minority representation in its work force. Even more relevant, there has been debate over whether a university must have sufficient minority representation in student admissions.''

''I see,'' said XT. ''Well, I'm sure the same debate over numerical goals and quotas will occur in the grade schools. Of course, this is nothing new, is it? Haven't you had plenty of controversy over racial balance in grade schools?''

"We certainly have," replied the host. "Busing to achieve racial balance has been required in many places, especially large cities. In fact, won't your plan undo the racial mixing that we have achieved?''

"How much mixing have you achieved?" asked XT. "Isn't it true that many whites live in suburbs and are not subject to the mixing that results from busing in the neighboring city?''

"That's true," replied the host.

"Actually," continued XT, "my voucher plan may achieve more mixing, on a voluntary basis, than you have today. Today, inner city parents are not permitted to send their children to suburban public schools. And they cannot afford private schools. But with vouchers, suburban public schools will have some vacancies, as some residents opt for other public or private schools, and school revenues will depend on tuitions. Many suburban public schools will now seek to admit some inner city youngsters. So some inner city children will be able to attend largely white suburban public and private schools.''

"But," replied the host, "suburban residents won't want their public school overwhelmed with a large influx of inner city kids.''

"I'm sure you're right," said XT. "But I'm not talking about a large influx. I'm only talking about a small fraction of the student body of a suburban school. After all, the local public school will still give first priority to local residents. And it will accept applicants from other suburban districts as well. Today, most suburban schools admit no inner city children. With vouchers they may take some, especially since they will depend on tuitions.''

"You know," replied the host, "if you're talking about a small fraction of the student body, I think you're right. Even today, a few suburban communities participate in the ABC ('A Better Chance') program. The community admits a small number of inner city youngsters to its high school. It raises money to pay for a dormitory and to cover the education cost. These suburbanites apparently want to do their share to offer a better chance. In fact, many believe it is good for their own children to experience some diversity.''

''But,'' interjected XT, ''few communities are willing or able to raise the money. My voucher plan would take care of the money. Now, some inner city parents would be able to pay the full tuition. So the ABC communities would be able to admit some more inner city students, and many other communities would be able to admit such students for the first time.''

''There still wouldn't be widespread mixing by race and economic class,'' noted the host.

''Perhaps,'' replied XT, ''but there would be more mixing than under your current system. And all the mixing would be voluntary, avoiding the turmoil that has accompanied some of your busing plans.''

''But,'' said the host, ''isn't there a negative side to this better chance for some inner city youngsters? What about the kids left behind in the inner city schools? Won't they be worse off? After all, who will take advantage of the opportunity to attend suburban schools? The most concerned parents. The kids who probably need a better chance most will remain behind. And they will no longer benefit from the positive influence of the best students, who have left for better schools.''

''The loss of some of the best students is a negative,'' conceded XT. ''But you are forgetting something. You are forgetting the new pressure on each inner city school that is now fighting, for the first time, for its financial survival. The schools have got to try to stop the exodus. So even the kids who stay behind will get better treatment. Remember my account of the diverse algebra and English classes. I think the odds are high that education will improve even for those who stay.''

''Let me turn to another objection to your plan,'' said the host. ''Many of us have always viewed our public schools as a melting pot. True, due to residential patterns, there is only limited mixing by race or economic class. But the public school usually does mix children from families who differ in religion and philosophy. Often, this mixing breeds mutual understanding, tolerance, and respect. Also, the public school assures that children are exposed to ideas and viewpoints they may not hear from their own parents.

"Under your voucher plan, won't most parents choose schools that closely reflect their own religion and philosophy? Because your vouchers go to households, not schools, our courts may decide that they can be used at accredited schools run by religious organizations, without violating our First Amendment. If this happens, isn't there a danger of less mutual understanding, tolerance, and respect in our society? And won't children be denied exposure to ideas and viewpoints that may differ from those of their parents?"

"You have indeed raised some tough questions," replied XT. "Let me do my best to reply. There seems to be no question that affluent people like to live in affluent neighborhoods and send their children to schools with other affluent children. That's what I see under your current system, and my voucher plan may actually provide a little more economic and racial mixing in schools than you've achieved under your public school system.

"But when I visit your neighborhoods, I see people with different philosophies and religions on the same block. They socialize together, and their kids play together. Would they really separate their children along religious or philosophical lines under a voucher system?"

"But," replied the host, "local public schools may be responsible for the current mixing. Kids meet in school, then they play together, and that's what you observe. The parents meet each other through their kids. So the public school pulls everyone together."

"True," replied XT, "and that's exactly why most public schools will hold their own under my voucher plan. Stimulated by the pressure of competition, they will perform better. And with better performance, they will continue to command support. The advantage of the local school will continue to be decisive for many parents."

"But," responded the host, "what about the parents who care most about religion or philosophy? Aren't they most likely to seek schools with their own kind? And aren't their children the ones that most need mixing and exposure?"

"That's a tough one," replied XT. "How you feel about this may depend on whether it's the education of your own children, or someone else's. May I take an example? I understand that this biological theory of evolution has caused some controversy in your schools. I must tell you, it would cause quite a stir in mine, because no one has thought of evolution on my planet. Personally, I am as fascinated with evolution as I am with competition.

"Now, I suspect that you have little sympathy with those parents who don't want their children exposed to this theory because they believe it undermines their religion?"

"I think their children should have the opportunity to learn modern science," replied the host.

"And you do not relish the thought that a voucher system would let these parents place their children in a school that omits the theory of evolution, correct?" asked XT.

"It's unfair to their children," answered the host.

"But now suppose the shoe were on the other foot. Suppose that these fundamentalists controlled the public schools, and were the majority. Wouldn't you be grateful for a voucher that let you place your children in a secular school that teaches evolution?"

"Of course," replied the host.

"But who are you to deny your children exposure?" asked XT.

"Exposure to what?" asked the host.

"Exposure to the comfort of a deep religious faith grounded in the Bible."

"I would feel constant anguish if I knew my children were being subjected to a biblical curriculum," replied the host with evident emotion. "After all, these are my children we're talking about."

"And that's how these fundamentalist parents feel today. You say they're denying their children the opportunity to learn modern science. But if they controlled the public schools, they would say that you are denying your children the comfort of religious faith. They feel anguish if their children attend the school you control. And you would feel anguish if your children attended the school they control."

"But the shoe isn't on the other foot," exclaimed the host with evident relief.

"True," replied XT. "But can you be sure it never will be? I have a question for you. Are you an insurance-minded person?"

"What do you mean?" asked the host.

"Do you get peace of mind from having adequate health, life, and auto insurance?"

"Certainly," replied the host. "But what's this got to do with your voucher plan?"

"Well," replied XT, "you can regard my voucher plan as insurance against the shoe being on the other foot. True, at this moment it looks doubtful that fundamentalists will achieve a significant impact on your public school curriculum. But can you be sure it will never happen? After all, if they are forced to stay within the public school system, they will fight hard to influence the content of textbooks and curriculum. As they see it, they are fighting for the moral lives of their own children. Their intensity may make up for their numbers."

"I suppose it's not impossible," admitted the host. "I know they could never control my town's school board. But, come to think of it, I'm not so sure they can't have an impact on my state government. And our public schools are constrained by state curriculum policy."

"My voucher plan does two things," continued XT. "First, it gives these fundamentalist parents an outlet. They can send their children to their own private schools, instead of being compelled to try to influence the curriculum of the public schools. Second, if the public school curriculum becomes unacceptable to you, you can afford to send your children to a private school. So my voucher plan really gives every family insurance against an adverse event—an unacceptable change in the public school curriculum."

"I had never looked at it that way," replied the host.

"I admit," continued XT, "that under the voucher plan, fewer children will be exposed to ideas or viewpoints that their parents don't like. You will regard this as disturbing when it comes to other children, but comforting when it comes to your own."

"But," asked the host, "won't there be less mutual understanding, tolerance, and respect in our society?"

"That's a hard one," replied XT. "True, some private schools may now give students the impression that their religion or philosophy is superior, and others are inferior. And some students may get less direct exposure to youngsters with other religious or philosophical views, and less contact with other ideas and viewpoints that might broaden their own horizons and understanding.

"But today, fundamentalist parents argue that public schools teach, implicitly or explicitly, that 'secular humanism' is best, and that fundamentalism is inferior. Today's battle over public school curriculum breeds antagonism and animosity on both sides.

"With the voucher plan," continued XT, "the current battle over public school curriculum would become less intense. The most committed fundamentalists would send their children to private schools, and pay less attention to public school textbooks and curriculum. And secularists would worry less about fundamentalists.

"In fact," said XT, "the voucher system itself would send a message that this society truly is based on mutual respect and tolerance. The message would be: I respect your right to choose a school for your children, and you respect mine. I may not agree with your philosophy, and you may not agree with mine, but we will respect each other's desire to choose a school that is compatible with our own philosophy."

"But isn't there a danger greater than mere differences in religion and philosophy?" countered the host. "Won't some schools preach intolerance and hatred?"

"Some may," replied XT. "But how many? After all, today everyone is free to congregate with 'his own kind' on Saturdays or Sundays in religious gatherings. And everyone is free to join political or philosophical groups and attend their meetings. Yet it is remarkable how little preaching of intolerance and hatred goes on in these religious or political gatherings. It appears that the overwhelming majority of Americans do not wish to hear such negative preaching."

"My dear XT," replied the host, "you seem a little naive. I'm afraid many Americans do harbor prejudices, especially religious and racial.''

"I'm sure you are right," replied XT. "But that's my point. Despite these prejudices, most still don't want to hear negative preaching in their religious or political gatherings. So despite these prejudices, I suspect that very few will choose schools that preach intolerance. Remember, even today, private schools are free to preach hatred. How many do?''

International competition

"But you can't deny that a voucher system would have its problems," said the host.

"Of course not," replied XT. "What doesn't have problems? But remember, you are engaged in an intense international competition over the future standard of living. And, forgive me for saying so, the current trend is not in your favor. To stay second to none, you must accumulate capital faster—human and knowledge, as well physical. You need better performance in your education sector. So the real question is this: Can you afford the luxury of doing without your best weapon for improving performance—the mechanism of competition?''

"But isn't education different?" asked the host.

"Yes," said XT, "it's more important.''

Notes

1. Milton Friedman, *Capitalism and Freedom* (Chicago: University of Chicago Press, 1962), p. 89.

2. Mine is a modification of the version considered by John Coons and Stephen Sugarman in *Education by Choice: The Case for Family Control* (Berkeley: University of California Press, 1978), p. 198.

3. To implement the variable voucher plan, the state government must either utilize a state personal income or consumption tax, or obtain access to the Federal Internal Revenue Service personal income or consumption tax data for its residents. Conversion of the personal tax, at the state or federal level, from income to consumption as advocated in chapter 3, would pose no obstacle; the variable voucher schedule could be based on either income or consumption, since the necessary income data would still be available on the tax return.

4. This section has benefited from Thomas Sowell, *Black Education: Myths and Tragedies* (New York: David McKay Company, Inc., 1972), pp. 242-50.

11

UNIVERSAL MAJOR-RISK
HEALTH INSURANCE

President Competitus had reason to be proud. His policies had kept the United States second to none economically. As his plane touched down in Stockholm for a meeting of economically advanced nations, he was radiant, eager for the press conference that would soon follow.

"What will they ask about first?" he said to his coterie of confident aides. "Will it be about our recent success in raising our saving rate? I can't wait."

As he entered the airport, the president was pleased to see the throng of foreign reporters, pushing and shoving to get near the microphone he would use for his press conference. Soon he was behind the microphone, smiling confidently.

"Ladies and gentlemen, I would be delighted to answer your questions."

"Mr. President," said a Swedish reporter, "why is it that your nation—among the richest on earth—permits thousands of citizens to be financially broken by medical bills, and millions to worry that the same thing might happen to them?"

For an instant, President Competitus was taken aback. He had not expected this question. But he recovered quickly.

"In the United States we believe that doctors and hospitals shouldn't be strangled by government regulation. We believe they should be free to practice medicine without government interference.''

''Perhaps so,'' responded the reporter, ''but my question was about paying bills, not the free practice of medicine. Why doesn't every citizen have enough health insurance to prevent financial disaster?''

President Competitus tried to remain unruffled. ''We have a fine private health insurance system. Many of our citizens obtain free hospital care.''

But the reporter persisted. ''I agree that your system takes care of the average person's routine hospital stay. But what about the exceptionally long hospital stay? Or the person with a chronic illness who needs outpatient and home care? And what about the person who is not average—for example, the person who works for a small business that doesn't provide health insurance, or the person who is between jobs and has no coverage? Isn't it true, Mr. President, that your system permits these citizens to suffer an unbearable financial burden due to a medical problem?''

The color was draining from President Competitus's face. He looked around for help. At that moment an aide earned his pay; he calmly took the microphone and said, ''The president would love to entertain more questions, but I'm afraid we are already late for our reception. There will be time for questions tomorrow. Thank you very much.''

With that, the aide unplugged the microphone, and led the president by the arm away from the throng. A half hour later, the president huddled with his advisers in a hotel suite high above Stockholm. He knew he would have to face the reporters again the next day.

''These Scandinavians are so damn righteous about their welfare state, especially about medical care. But maybe they're right,'' he said. ''Maybe medical care should be free for everyone. Maybe our government should pay everyone's entire medical bill.''

It happened that the president's inner circle included a health economist who, needless to say, immediately spoke up.

"Mr. President, that would be a serious mistake. I agree that our lack of universal protection against financial disaster is shameful. But we shouldn't go to the other extreme. After all, you do remember the Aroman Food Crisis, don't you?"

"The Aroman Food Crisis?" everyone asked all at once. No one had ever heard of it. From his briefcase, the health economist pulled out what appeared to be an old manuscript.

"The hour is late," he said. "Tomorrow morning we can begin to develop a national policy for health insurance. Tonight, relax, and let me read to you from this ancient text. I assure you it will prove helpful when we get down to business tomorrow morning."

And so he began to read.

The Aroman Food Crisis[1]

I

An ancient proverb warns, "There is no such thing as a free lunch." Yet many years ago, in the land of Aroma, there emerged a free-wheeling, spirited, well-intentioned people, confident that food could, and should, be free. On a historic day, the Aroman Senate rose to its finest hour, and passed the long-awaited Free Food Act. Lest the title mislead you, in a dramatic amendment before final passage, Senator Inebriatus, with an impassioned though rambling oration, won the inclusion of all beverages under the act.

The passage of the Free Food Act (FFA) had been inspired by the tragic plight of those Aromans with enormous nutritional requirements—fortunately, only a small fraction of the citizenry. But when the Senate's work was done, the act had gone well beyond these citizens. For under the act, food and drink were free for all Aromans. No longer would any Aroman face even the smallest "barrier" to food and drink. In other words, no longer would any Aroman have to pay for what he consumed.

Never again would any Aroman be seen in the marketplace

trying to decide whether a luscious honeydew melon was worth its price. Nor would the marketplace be degraded by haggling and bargaining between stubborn buyers and sellers. Now, there would only be smiles. "Take as much as you want," was the refrain that abounded. "My price is not for you, my friend, but for our beloved government." Word spread to other lands about the pleasant vibrations of the Aroman marketplace.

Yet it was not the gaiety of the marketplace that caused the most excitement in distant lands. Most wondrous of all were the spectacular public banquets that soon became an everyday feature of Aroman life. Soon after the FFA was passed, banquet halls sprang up throughout Aroma. Aromans had always taken a large midday meal. But now, in retrospect, those meals seemed like a "quick lunch" by comparison.

Each banquet hall manager boasted of serving only "the finest," regardless of cost. When one government regulator asked the manager of the Endless Lobster, perhaps the most renowned hall in all Aroma, if perhaps his place was not a bit extravagant, the manager's reply was angry: "Are you suggesting that I sacrifice quality? I would rather be banished from Aroma than offer second-class food and drink." The government regulator was reported to have hung his head in shame, and then apologize profusely.

And so, the early days of the Free Food Act were joyous, heady ones for the Aromans.

II

But alas, this happy Aroman scene did not last long. Indeed, to the dismay of many Aromans, the country was soon on the brink of disaster. While food and drink were free to each Aroman, someone, of course, had to pay the bill. Now, it was no surprise to the average Aroman that it was the government who was supposed to pay food sellers in the marketplace and the banquet halls. Indeed, it was the cry, "The government should pay!" that rang in the ears of Aroman senators when they passed the FFA.

What surprised the average Aroman was the government's announcement that, in order to honor its financial obligations to the food providers, it would have to raise the taxes of each Aroman citizen.

Even more shocking than the imposition of the new Food Tax was its astounding size. The tax came to five times as much per meal per person as the average Aroman had spent before the FFA. The reason, said the government spokesman, was simple: the average Aroman was now selecting food and drink of such quality and quantity, that the cost per meal was now five times as great.

The Aroman Senate responded to the crisis. It held hearings on the Incredible Overutilization, as it was called. So vivid were the accounts of the banquet hall abuses, that senators were regularly given the ancient potion Alka-Seltzer. In angry testimony, taxpayers testified that banquet hall managers did nothing to control costs. They simply passed their exorbitant expenses on to the government, which reimbursed them, no questions asked.

Amid the furor, the Senate acted. The answer, said the committee report, was to negotiate prices, and establish a limited budget, in advance, with each banquet hall and food seller.

"Since we are spending five times as much on food and drink as we should be," stated the Senate committee report, "we will simply appropriate only one-fifth of our current expenditure. Within this limit, we will allocate our budget on a regional basis. In each region, we will enter into agreements with each food provider. Once agreement is reached, the banquet hall will get no more than the amount specified in the agreement for the year, no matter how great its costs.

"With a firm regulatory hand," the report concluded, "we will control costs without retreating from the sacred principle that the individual must face absolutely no financial barrier to food and drink."

On leaving the Senate chamber, one senator said with a confident smile, "If we refuse to appropriate any more money, then we can't spend more, can we? The food cost crisis is over."

III

But the trouble was only beginning. Yes, the expenditure ceiling ended the cost crisis. But it produced a crisis that many Aromans felt was far worse. As the end of the fiscal year approached, food for the country nearly ran out. Aromans were faced with starvation. How did it happen?

It happened because banquet halls and food suppliers reached their negotiated limits well before the year was over. Except for the price control, and a budget ceiling on each provider, the new amendment changed nothing else. Aromans continued to order the finest food and drink. With food still free to each Aroman, there was no reason for the average Aroman to change his behavior. Aroman waiters continued to encourage the highest quality, regardless of cost. As for the banquet hall managers, they looked forward to a fine vacation during the last months of the year.

"I can reach my reimbursement ceiling in nine months," said one banquet manager. "Why should I reduce our quality and style? My customers want the finest, in abundant quantities, and I am proud to satisfy them. Let someone else plan for the end of the year. I and my fine professional staff will enjoy a well-earned vacation."

After a gluttonous fall and winter, Aromans struggled through the spring near starvation, desperately awaiting the new fiscal year, which in those days began in July. Many affluent Aromans were still able to obtain food, thanks to an illegal market. Aroman entrepreneurs, anticipating the shortage, had stockpiled free food during the fall and winter, and now sold it at high prices to those able to pay. But many other Aromans suffered. Meanwhile, new hearings were held in the Senate, where the mood was one of sober realism.

"It is obvious," said one senator, "that unless we directly control the practice of each food seller and banquet hall, budget ceilings will continue to produce disaster. We cannot limit the total expenditure unless we also carefully control the individual expenditures that eventually constitute the total."

It was now clear that the annual budget negotiation with each provider would have to become detailed, indeed. The provider's entire mode of operation would have to be carefully scrutinized before the ceiling was fixed. Each provider would have to be kept under constant surveillance to make sure that it complied with the budget agreement. But how could this be done effectively?

"We need to review utilization at each banquet hall," asserted one senator. "If they keep serving exotic food and liquor, we'll threaten to cut off their funds."

This was met by a disdainful glare from the chefs and waiters in the gallery. Then Intimidatus, the president of the Aroman Maitre d's' Association (AMA), which also represented chefs and ordinary waiters, addressed the Senate committee. His dignified manner and white hair, seeming to symbolize wisdom and responsibility, filled the Senate with awe. Intimidatus calmly pointed out that many of the items on the menus of the finest banquet halls were modern nutritional necessities.

He then referred to these items, analyzing each, leaving the senators confused, but impressed with his abstruse terminology. "Yes, in some cases they are not necessary, and may even be harmful. But in others, the very life of the individual is at stake. If laymen are allowed to interfere with the professional judgment of trained waiters who advise citizens what to order, lives will be jeopardized."

Needless to say, a chill ran through the Senate chamber. "You waiters and chefs who are properly trained in nutrition," Senator Conciliatus blurted out, "are the only ones qualified to judge what each individual requires. Only you can separate unnecessary overutilization from genuine necessity. I therefore propose that we establish Professional Standards Review Organizations in each area. Let's call them PSROs. They will be composed exclusively of trained waiters and chefs, who will review the practices of each banquet hall. The PSRO will recommend when funds should be cut because waste is occurring." The proposal was greeted enthusiastically by other senators.

Their glee was interrupted, however, when the president of the

AMA asked, "I trust that the PSRO will also be charged with making sure that the highest quality standards are preserved at all banquet halls?" While the senators nodded uneasily, they wondered whether a PSRO would try to keep cost down as much as it would try to keep quality and style up. "What would you concentrate on, if you were a chef or waiter on a PSRO?" one senator asked another nervously.

"The trouble with the PSRO," said Senator Consumus, rising to his feet, "is that it has only waiters and chefs. Of course it won't be tough enough. We need strong consumer representation on these review boards. Then we'll get action."

For the first time since the debate began, Senator Economus asked to be recognized. "Consumus, how carefully will your board review each case, and how many will they examine?"

"Oh," replied Consumus, "they will surely review most cases, and each very carefully."

"Surely, Consumus, you realize what that would cost? There are thousands of cases. We would be wasting an important fraction of our labor force serving on review boards, instead of producing goods and services."

Though momentarily dismayed, Consumus quickly regained his composure. "Well, then they will review only a small number of cases, but will do these carefully. After all, this is the method of our respected Internal Revenue Service. The fear of review will make all waiters act properly."

"I'm afraid that there is a basic difference between the taxpayer and the waiter," responded Economus. "For the taxpayer, there is relatively little discretion. The rules say what he must count as his income, and what he must pay. If he is caught with a major discrepancy, he may argue, but almost always to no avail. Our IRS will not hesitate to punish him when his crime is clear. It is this willingness to punish because the crime is clear that makes our taxpayers afraid, and makes most of them comply without our direct oversight.

"Our waiter," Economus continued, "is in a very different position. Only in the most scandalous cases will his actions clearly be a crime. With so much judgment involved in serving an individual's nutritional needs, with even our most expert waiters disagreeing over what is most appropriate, punishment in most cases would be most unfair. In the overwhelming majority of cases, therefore, the review board will at most reprimand the waiter, and warn against future excesses. Do you think most waiters will change their ways because there is a small chance that they might be slapped on the wrist?''

An expression of gloom came over the senators' faces.

Consumus grew more flustered. "Then the board will have to show the courage to impose a severe penalty. If the description of the case looks suspicious, the board will just have to act."

At this, Economus rose to his feet. "Are you saying, Consumus, that if a waiter and his customer, based on the particular nutritional history and needs of this customer, after extensive consultation and examination, decide that certain food and drink are necessary, that your board, based on a descriptive account, will overrule their decision?"

"How else will we get results?" replied Consumus with exasperation. "Of course, they will have the right to appeal."

"But," continued Economus, "if your appeal board conducts a careful investigation, this will once again be very expensive. Virtually everyone will appeal, since much is at stake. If your appeal board processes cases without such investigation, and at low cost, it will be little better than the review board in the first place. An outside board, with far less information about the customer's special needs, will impose its decision on the customer and waiter."

"Well," replied Consumus, "what's so wrong with that? As long as consumers constitute a majority on the board, they'll watch out for the customer's needs. After all, how can consumer representatives be harmful to individual consumers?"

"By not having sufficient on-the-scene information, Consumus, to make the decision with the sensitivity that is required. Yes, they may be right some of the time, when excessive food and drink has been ordered. But what about the other cases, where what was ordered was truly necessary, but the review board is simply unable to investigate carefully enough to realize this. I suppose those individuals, with perhaps their very lives at stake, are just out of luck.''

''That's the price we'll have to pay,'' Consumus responded, defiant, yet uneasy.

Another senator now turned to a different aspect of the problem. ''We are building too many banquet halls, with facilities and equipment that are far too extravagant for our needs. This must end.'' His plea obviously struck a responsive chord. ''I propose,'' he continued, ''that every new banquet hall, and every expansion of a current one be required to obtain a 'Certificate of Need' from the government before it can proceed.''

Economus slowly rose to his feet. ''You will do more harm than good if you limit facilities and equipment without changing individual utilization. It's the same as thinking that a spending ceiling can end the problem.''

''But why?'' asked Senator Naivus. Other senators turned uneasily to hear Economus's explanation, glad that Senator Naivus, as usual, had asked the question for them.

''Suppose,'' began Economus, ''that according to your rational planning, you think there are already enough banquet halls, kitchen facilities, and so on, in some area. How did you decide this? By calculating how much would be needed if each person ate reasonably, and only those with special nutritional requirements ordered expensive food. But suppose people don't eat reasonably. Suppose they continue to eat and drink the way they are doing today. Then you'll run out of capacity, under your plan, and we'll have another emergency. Some of our people will wine and dine extravagantly as usual. But many others won't be able to get a table at any banquet hall, because there will be no room. And someone who truly needs a special food will find that the special kitchen facilities are being used to prepare that food for someone who is ordering it as a luxury.''

Most dismayed by what Economus said was Senator Regulatus. He countered, ''Economus, if our ability to regulate is really so feeble, then why are our people satisfied with our great public utilities, which my committee oversees? For example, our water utility company distributes water, and our fuel utility company, fuel, to every Aroman home. We regulate the price each charges, and few citizens complain.''

"What you are forgetting," Economus answered, "is that every Aroman home must pay for the water and fuel it consumes. So people only use what they need, and no more. That's why there is no serious problem. With our utility companies, we have to regulate the price they charge, because they're monopolies. But we don't have to regulate utilization, because people do that themselves since they have to pay for whatever they use. That's the crucial difference.''

After a long silence in the chamber, another senator asked the final question to Economus. ''Are you saying that trying to regulate efficiency through utilization review, certificate of need, spending ceilings, prospective reimbursement, and other requirements, may well do more harm than good?''

"That is exactly what I'm saying," Economus replied.

IV

"If we can't regulate banquet halls, and marketplace food stands," said Senator Socialus, "then let's take them over and run them ourselves, on behalf of the people." Proposals by Senator Socialus were usually viewed with suspicion by other senators. But now, out of desperation, they listened. "First, we'll put all the chefs, waiters, and maitre d's on salary, and stop paying them in proportion to the cost of the food and drink they serve. That will end their incentive to encourage overordering." Many senators nodded, and Socialus continued. "We'll have rational planning of facilities and food production. This is the only way we can solve our problem." While the proposal was radical, many senators seemed to feel it might be the only course left.

But then Economus spoke up. "How will the budget for a

banquet hall, and the salaries of those who run them, be determined?''

Socialus answered, ''Our government will decide these matters on behalf of the people. We will create a Ministry of Food and Drink to administer this sector of our economy.''

Economus responded, ''If the Ministry of Food and Drink, rather than consumers, determines the financial success of these providers, then it is the Ministry, not their customers, that they will have an incentive to please.''

''But Economus,'' replied Socialus, ''the Ministry will only reward providers who please their customers.''

''How will the Ministry know who these are?'' Economus asked.

''Well,'' answered Socialus, ''we might take surveys of customers. Or better yet, we could see which providers are greatly in demand, and which are not.''

''There is a problem with your method,'' said Economus. ''Since consumers pay nothing, they will prefer the banquet halls and food stands where they are allowed to order as much as they want. The most popular providers will probably be the most wasteful. Surely you will not reward their popularity with higher budgets and salaries.''

''Of course not,'' Socialus responded, ''but we will evaluate them, don't you worry.''

''Then I must repeat,'' said Economus, ''that it will be the evaluators, not customers, whom each provider will be most eager to please. This raises a still more serious problem. Do you realize how many banquet halls and food stands there are in Aroma?''

''Thousands of them,'' interrupted Naivus, who had been listening intently, along with the other senators.

''How will the Ministry oversee, evaluate, and administer all of these efficiently?'' continued Economus.

''Why, the Ministry will have to be given the manpower it needs to do the job. We must have administrators in each local community, who will be responsible for all providers in that area.

They will in turn report to regional administrators, who in turn will report to the Ministry itself. We will have constant communication between the bottom and top of our hierarchy.''

"Have you estimated the cost of employing these full-time administrators?'' asked Economus.

"No,'' answered Socialus, "but the cost of justice is surely worth bearing.''

"Unless the same justice can be achieved far more cheaply,'' replied Economus, and he continued to warm to his task. "When it is budget time, will your local administrators be advocates for their providers, or be representatives of the Ministry?''

"They will represent the Ministry, of course,'' answered Socialus. "They must recommend that their superior providers be rewarded, and the inferior ones, penalized.''

"Are you sure it will not work the other way around?'' said Economus. "For example, if most of the providers in an area do a poor job, do you really expect the administrator to recommend that funds for his area be cut?'' Socialus replied saying yes, this was the administrator's duty. Economus continued, "There is a problem here. If you do not reward area administrators according to the performance of their providers, what incentive do they have to strive to improve service in their area? On the other hand, if you do reward them on that basis, they will have an incentive to become advocates for their providers, defending their performance before the Ministry. You will have great difficulty judging provider performance.''

"Economus, your trouble is that you always assume financial incentives are everything. Our administrators will realize that they are servants of the people. They will act accordingly, and strive to make the system work for people's needs.''

"Socialus, my good friend, I do not think that financial incentives are everything. But I'm afraid I have seen too much in my time to agree with you that they are nothing. And there is something else about your plan that disturbs me,'' continued Economus. "Suppose an area has a poor administrator, and providers in that area give poor service. They are discourteous to customers, whom they have little incentive to please as long as the budget keeps funding them; they often keep people waiting in lines for tables, and offer a poor assortment of low-quality dishes. Socialus, what recourse do the people of this area have?''

"I expected a more difficult problem, my dear Economus," answered Socialus confidently. "Obviously, they can complain to the Ministry. In fact, we will do better. In each area, we will set up consumer councils. It will be their responsibility to take the complaints of citizens to the Ministry. Citizens will have the opportunity, at last, to participate directly in governing the institutions that control their lives.''

"I'm afraid, my dear Socialus, that your answer does not satisfy me. Surely, this will be a time-consuming process. The administrators and providers will defend themselves. It will require a sustained campaign by local citizens and their councils to achieve results. Perhaps some citizens will enjoy the battle. The vast majority, however, want nothing more than good service. Indeed, they do not wish to spend their time attending consumer council meetings, or writing letters to the Ministry.''

"Then they must learn to like direct participation and the democratic process,'' replied Socialus.

"In the meantime," Economus went on, "until they have won a change, these unlucky Aromans will have nowhere to turn. Socialus, there is something most ironic here. You are famous for your reputation as an ardent foe of private monopolies, which leave consumers no choice. And yet your plan would turn our whole food and drink sector into one giant monopoly. To be sure, it would be a public monopoly. But like any monopoly, dissatisfied consumers would have nowhere to go.''

"Economus, are you unable to see the difference between a private monopoly, whose motive is greed, and a Ministry whose wish is to serve the people?''

"I see how, in one respect, they are different," Economus replied. "But Socialus, can you see how, in another respect, they are also the same?''

Seeing that this question was in vain, Economus now proceeded to his final point.

V

"I have a final concern about your proposal, Socialus. It applies not only to your plan, however, but to any Free Food Act that would finance most or all purchases of food and drink through our government budget. Of all the arguments I have made in the course of this Senate debate, I believe this one may be the most telling of all. You see, so far my arguments for efficiency have struck some of you as lacking in compassion, and perhaps have therefore left you cold. What I am about to say, however, should at last impress those of you whose sole concern is social justice. For I will now explain why, contrary to the humanitarian intentions of the supporters of the Free Food Act, its effects will be to harm, not help, those Aromans whose needs are greatest—our poor, and our elderly."

A silence fell on the Senate chamber. Loyal supporters of the Free Food Act, famed for their devotion to programs for the poor and the elderly, turned their attention to Economus for the first time, their countenances reflecting disbelief and concern. The debate had clearly reached its climax, and Economus's ability to defend his assertion seemed likely to decide the outcome.

"As you know," he continued solemnly, "our citizens are unwilling to be taxed without limit. In a dictatorship, where the ruler decides the taxes and people pay them without a whimper for fear of the ruler's wrath, people's sentiments would be no obstacle. But in our Aroman democracy, the situation is very different. We senators must heed the people's wishes, or soon find that others have been elected to replace us.

"Before passing this act, no taxes were needed to finance food and drink. We could therefore devote the taxes we raised to tasks that only our government can effectively perform—like helping our poor and our elderly. If we must now use taxes to finance all food and drink expenditures—an enormous sum—then we will be unable to continue these vital tasks with the same generosity. It is our poor, and our elderly, who will be harmed the most by the reduction in our other government expenditures. Surely the senators who support full tax financing of food and drink do not realize that its unintended effect would be to shift government spending away from the poor and elderly toward middle- and upper-income Aromans, most of whom can afford to pay their own food bills. I am afraid that the Free Food Act is a sad example of how good intentions can at times lead to harmful results.''

A long and sober silence was finally broken by the sound of the gavel of the president of the Senate as he adjourned the session.

VI

When the session opened the next day, Naivus was the first to speak. ''What shall we do, Economus?'' he asked. As usual, he voiced the question then on the minds of most senators.

''My proposal is very simple,'' answered Economus, ''and I am only too glad to set it before you today. First, we must have compassion for those unfortunate Aromans who have enormous nutritional requirements, and simply cannot afford to pay for most of the food and drink they need. We should place a limit, that varies according to the citizen's income, on the out-of-pocket expense that any Aroman must pay for the food and drink he requires. Once a person reaches the limit, our Aroman government should pay the rest. However, the limit would be set high enough so that only those with truly serious needs would reach it. Let's call my proposal income-related major-risk national food insurance.

''It could be easily implemented through our personal income tax. When an Aroman files his annual income tax return, he reports his annual income to our IRS. Using this information, our government can decide each Aroman's maximum burden. For convenience, our government will initially pay every food bill. When an Aroman buys food, he will simply use a government food credit card with his stamped Social Security number. The provider will send the bill to the government for payment. But then the government will immediately bill the Aroman for the amount he owes, according to his income.

"Fortunately, only a relatively small fraction of Aromans are forced to spend more than that critical fraction of their income on food and drink. Thus, the amount of tax we must raise to help these Aromans is much smaller than the amount required by the Free Food Act. We will therefore be able to continue, and even increase, our government programs to assist the poor and the elderly.

"At the same time, waste and inefficiency will be greatly reduced. Once again, the average Aroman will want to weigh the benefit of anything he orders against its cost. This will automatically limit wasteful overordering, without regulation.

"True, Aromans will continue to rely on trained waiters to advise them concerning their nutritional needs, and the food and beverages they require. But our citizens will now communicate to their waiters their concern that the cost be reasonable. Waiters will realize that citizens who incur an excessive food bill will be less able to afford a generous tip. Moreover, citizens will seek waiters who show concern for their pocketbook, as well as their nutrition. Waiters who indulge their 'technological imperative'— who recommend the most technologically sophisticated food preparation without regard to cost or true necessity— will find themselves losing customers. Managers and waiters at extravagant banquet halls will watch, with dismay, as citizens seek prudent waiters at rival halls that provide sufficient quality at far less cost.

"Thus, under my simple proposal, no Aroman will be bankrupted by his nutritional requirements; waste and inefficiency will be largely curtailed without cumbersome and costly regulation; and we will conserve scarce tax dollars so that they can be spent to assist the poor and the elderly in other ways."

When Economus had said this, he thanked the senators for listening, and sat down. Unfortunately, here the tattered manuscript recounting the Aroman food crisis becomes illegible, and to this day we do not know whether the Aroman senate followed his advice.

Having completed his recounting of the ancient story, the president's health economist looked up. Everyone was sound asleep except the president, who nodded his head drowsily with a sign of approval. Within seconds, he too was asleep.

An unlikely hero:
The Internal Revenue Service

The next morning, the president asked what to do about medical coverage, and his health economist responded.

"We should follow Economus's advice. Every household should be automatically provided with a major-risk health insurance policy in which each person's maximum burden is scaled to his income.[2] First, we will need to decide the yearly maximum financial burden we will permit at each income level. For example:

Household Income	Maximum Burden	(% of income)
$20,000	$1,200	6%
$60,000	$4,800	8%
$100,000	$10,000	10%

"Second, we must decide the patient 'cost sharing (co-payment) rate'—the fraction that the patient must pay, at each income level, before he reaches his maximum burden. To illustrate:

Household Income	Rate
$20,000	10%
$60,000	30%
$100,000	50%

"For example, if in a given year the $20,000 household incurs a $6,000 medical bill, it would pay 10 percent, or $600, and the government would pay the rest. If its bill were $12,000, it would pay 10 percent, or $1,200. But now that it has reached its maximum burden, any additional medical bill would be completely paid by the government."

"But," interjected the president, "how do you decide the patient cost sharing rate for each income level?"

"Our aim," responded the health economist, "is to move toward *income neutrality* in medical care. We want to reduce the influence of income as a determinant of medical care. We want to set the rate at each income level so that the low-, middle-, and high-income person with the same disease and the same desire for medical care can obtain roughly the same care."

"But," asked the president, "how can you know, in advance, the rate table that will achieve income neutrality in medical care?"

"We can't," replied the health economist. "Of course, we can use some statistical studies of household medical expenditures to make our initial table. But then we will need to adjust the tables periodically based on experience. If any income class has below-average expenditures, and there is no indication that the discrepancy is based on less need or desire for medical care, then its cost sharing rate should be reduced. Of course, our cost sharing rate structure will never hit it perfectly. But we will come close enough to satisfy any practical citizen who believes in moving toward income neutrality in medical care."

"Say," mused the president, "your scheme reminds me of our variable voucher proposal for education, where we also tried to move toward income neutrality by essentially the same method."

"Very good," exclaimed the health economist. "You're exactly right. Although most citizens have never heard the phrase 'income neutrality,' many believe we should move toward it in both education and medical care. These citizens feel that it's okay for expenditures on furniture, appliances, and clothes to depend heavily on income, but not expenditures on education and medical care. And you are correct that our method of approaching income neutrality is the same in both cases: vary the price directly with income so that the lower the household's income, the lower the price it faces."

"But," asked the president, "how do we implement such an income-related health insurance policy?"

"Are you ready for an unlikely hero?" asked the health economist. "What is the only agency in our country that has confidential information on nearly every household's income? The good old Internal Revenue Service. It's inescapable. The IRS is the key to achieving income neutrality. Here's how the policy would work.

"When the household files its tax return each year, a table included in the return would indicate its cost sharing rate and maximum burden for the coming year. For example, as it files its return, the $20,000 household would note that its cost sharing rate will be 10 percent, and its maximum burden, $1,200, in the coming year. Based on its tax return, the government would assign a cost sharing rate and maximum burden to each household for the coming year.[3]

"Whenever the household incurs a medical bill, it would pay with a government health credit card stamped with its Social Security number. The provider would then send the bill to the government. The government would pay the provider—physician or hospital—and bill the household according to its cost sharing rate. For example, if the $20,000 household incurs a $6,000 hospital bill, it would be billed for 10 percent, or $600."

"Am I right," asked the president, "that you want each household to pay a fraction of its medical bill, so it has an incentive to weigh benefit against cost? You want to avoid the Aroman problems, don't you? You don't like our current situation, where the average household has its entire hospital bill paid by its insurer, because then neither the patient, physician, or hospital has any reason to care about cost, and we have to impose cumbersome government regulation to try to cope with the symptoms of free hospital care."

"Exactly," answered the health economist.

"But what's to prevent a household from obtaining private insurance to cover the fraction that the government won't pay, so that hospital care stays free?" asked the president.

"Good question, Mr. President. Fortunately, the answer is simple. Under my proposal, the government won't pay anything if the person receives reimbursement from private insurance.''

"What do you mean?'' said the president.

"Simply this. When the provider sends the bill to the government, it must indicate that it is not submitting the bill to a private insurer, and must enclose the patient's signature making the same pledge.''

"But then,'' asked the president, "why would a household want to buy private health insurance, when it now gets this major-risk policy automatically?''

"The answer, Mr. President, is that it almost certainly wouldn't. In fact, there is another reason why the household wouldn't buy private insurance. My proposal includes removing the current tax subsidy for private health insurance. Today, when an employer pays $2,000 to buy an employee insurance, the employee is not taxed on the $2,000. Obviously, if the employee received the $2,000 as cash, he would be taxed on it. So we encourage compensation to go to health insurance. But once we provide every household with major-risk protection, there is no reason to continue this tax subsidy. So it would be eliminated.''

"What would happen at the workplace?'' asked the president.

"Most employees, Mr. President, would ask their employer to give them cash—say $2,000—instead of buying them private health insurance they no longer need. So each employee would obtain cash that used to go to a private insurance premium. This cash would help the employee to pay the tax increase the government must levy to finance its new insurance policy.''

"Which would be greater?'' asked the president. "The employee's cash saving from the premium, or the tax increase?''

"For the average employee, the cash saving from the premium would be greater, because the government must raise only enough revenue to pay part of the employee's hospital bill, while the private insurer needs to raise enough revenue to pay virtually the entire hospital bill. Also, the lower a household's income, the more the cash saving would exceed its tax increase. Why? Because a private insurer's premium is the same per household—say $2,000—regardless of the household's income, since the private insurer must cover each household's expected cost. But when we raise tax revenue, we do it according to ability to pay, so the tax increase on the low-income household is less, in dollars, than on the high-income household.

"But," worried the president, "the private insurance companies would no longer be selling much health insurance. I'm going to have a political problem with this. Won't these companies receive a serious jolt?"

"Yes, but not as much as you fear, Mr. President. There was the same fear in the 1960s when Medicare for the elderly was enacted. But the government contracted with private insurance companies to handle bill processing under Medicare. So the insurance companies retained their employees to continue bill processing. The companies were no longer paid for being insurers, but they continued to be paid for being the bill processors. They adjusted to the change very nicely."

"So," asked the president, "would the government contract with these companies to handle the bill processing?"

"Exactly, Mr. President. Why should the government try to process bills in-house when an experienced apparatus exists in the private insurance companies? The government will provide the companies with each household's maximum burden and cost sharing rate, based on the most recent tax return. But the bill processing will actually be performed by the private companies. Not only that, the companies will bid competitively for the government contracts, so the bill processing task will be 'privatized' even though the government is the insurer."

"That sounds much better," said the president. "Still, it would be even nicer for me, politically, if the private companies could continue selling the insurance itself."

"Unfortunately, Mr. President, there's no way to do that and accomplish our objectives. It's crucial to understand why. Private insurance cannot offer cost sharing that varies with *household* income. Why not? The private insurers cannot get data on *household* income from employers. True, the employer might provide each employee's wage, but he cannot provide data on the spouse's earnings, or the household's property income, unless the employee turns over his tax return. But what private insurer, competing for business, is going to request that employees turn over their tax returns?

"So any cost sharing must be uniform. And uniform cost sharing is inevitably too burdensome for unhealthy low-income households. Employers and unions know this, so on behalf of their employees, they obtain insurance with little or no cost sharing. The public, quite rightly, will never accept significant patient cost sharing unless it is income-related, with an ironclad maximum burden. And private insurance simply cannot offer this kind of cost sharing.

"But with virtually no patient cost sharing, as the Aromans learned, the result must be wasteful utilization and cumbersome government regulation of providers. The only way to limit waste and regulation is cost sharing. The only cost sharing that is equitable is income-related cost sharing. And the only one who can easily obtain household income data is the Internal Revenue Service.

"So, Mr. President, we cannot solve our problem as long as we rely on private insurance, because private insurance can never achieve income neutrality. Fortunately, as we saw when Medicare came in, the private insurers are needed to handle the bill processing. They will have a major role to play, and will be compensated accordingly. The tax increase must cover this bill processing cost, just as today's health insurance premiums cover the same cost."

"Now," said the president, "let me ask a more basic question. The Aroman lesson is persuasive for food. But will patient cost sharing really work for medical care? Will the heart attack victim look up from the stretcher and whisper, 'This hospital charges too much. Take me somewhere else'?"

"Mr. President, if the patient cost sharing strategy depended on economizing during emergencies, it would obviously fail. But it doesn't depend on this at all."

"Then how is it supposed to work?" asked the president.

"We don't want to limit emergency care. But we don't want a

tenth day in the hospital if it's not necessary. Who should make this decision? After all, some tenth days are very necessary. If it is free to the patient, then he and his doctor have no reason to weigh the cost—several hundred dollars—against the benefit. So government regulation must come in and apply pressure, as it does under Medicare's DRG (diagnostic related group) system.

"But suppose, Mr. President, that the patient must pay a fraction of the cost of the tenth day—a fraction that is scaled to his income. Then the government doesn't need to apply pressure. He and his doctor will weigh benefit against cost."

"But," asked the president, "doesn't the doctor really make the decision? Why should he care about the financial impact on his patient?"

"True, Mr. President, during an emergency the patient is preoccupied with his medical problem, and the doctor is often completely in charge. Even when the emergency passes, and the tenth day is weighed, the doctor may unilaterally make the decision. Today, the doctor usually knows that his patient will probably never see the hospital bill, much less pay any of it. But under our proposed insurance policy, the doctor will soon learn that his patient cares about the hospital bill. The recovering patient, with the emergency behind him, may well question the necessity of a tenth day and the doctor who prescribed it. Even now, doctors are often eager to show patients that they care about them, and try to save them money when this can be done without sacrificing quality. Under our policy, they will do the same with nonemergency hospital decisions."

"I have a final, fundamental question," said the president. "Why should people like paying a fraction of every medical bill? Won't they prefer free medical care?"

"Mr. President, remember what we learned from Aroma. Sure, it seems nice to get something for free. But each person should recognize that if it's free, government regulation of choice becomes inevitable. We see it already today. Under Medicare's DRG system, the government pressures hospitals to pressure doctors and patients to shorten hospital stays by fixing the government's payment according to the diagnosis, regardless of the actual cost incurred.

"So free care, Mr. President, is not really free. It inevitably brings on regulation, and the patient is no longer completely free to choose. The patient must wonder whether the doctor is deciding what is best medically, or bowing to the pressure of hospital administrators, who in turn are succumbing to the pressure of government regulators.

"Only patient cost sharing can eliminate government pressure. With cost sharing, government can let patients and doctors make unpressured decisions, because they have an incentive to weigh cost as well as benefit."

"But can we make people understand that?" asked the president.

"Perhaps not immediately," answered the health economist. "But people will like having a maximum burden. And they will like getting cash—say $2,000—when private insurance is no longer necessary, even though we will tax part of it away to finance our new insurance policy. So, Mr. President, many people will still support this proposal, even if they don't yet grasp its most important advantage: preserving each patient's freedom to choose medical care without governmental interference."

The press conference

The president once again stood before the microphone. But this time he took the offensive. He announced his new health insurance proposal, and let his health economist describe the details.

"Then everyone will have a maximum burden that relates to his income?" asked the same Swedish reporter with some hesitation.

"Yes," smiled the president.

"And there will be no gaps? The coverage will be universal, regardless of the person's job, or even whether he or she has a job?"

"Yes," answered the president. There was a long pause. Finally, with warmth in his voice, the president said, "I would be glad to talk more about it. Shall I?"

But the European reporters hesitated. Their enthusiasm from the previous day had vanished. For so many years, they had proudly asked Americans how the affluent United States could let people be financially broken by medical problems. And now, suddenly, the question had become obsolete. At last, the United States appeared on the way to being second to none in health insurance protection.

The reporters looked at each other. Finally, one raised his hand, and spoke when the president called on him.

"Mr. President, perhaps you might tell us how your country has achieved such a high saving rate?"

Notes

1. This fable originally appeared as an article: Laurence Seidman, "The Aroman Food Crisis: A Fable with a Lesson for National Health Insurance," *Medical Care* 16 (May 1978), 417-25.

2. This proposal was first set out by Martin Feldstein in "A New Approach to National Health Insurance," *The Public Interest* 23 (Spring 1971), 93–105.

3. If the household tax has been converted from income to consumption, as advocated in chapter 3, then the medical expenditure table can be based on either consumption or income. Even under a consumption tax, the income data would be available from the tax return.

12

PREPARE FOR THE Nth COUNTRY THREAT AND DETER THE SOVIET UNION

America's economic future cannot be saved unless our defense policy succeeds. None of the policies discussed in this book will matter much if we make a major mistake in our defense strategy. Contemplate, for a moment, the ruined economies of Europe in 1918, or Europe and Asia in 1945. To protect our economic future, we must avoid a major war while preserving our freedom.

Today's defense debate focuses primarily on the Soviet Union. The Kremlin certainly deserves our attention, and I will devote much of this chapter to the problem of deterring the Soviets in the coming decades.

But I want to begin with a different threat, one that may prove more ominous, but does not receive the priority it warrants. Moreover, it has decisive implications for our defense planning.

The Nth country threat

Every night on the news we hear of the actions of individuals, somewhere in the world, who appear willing to threaten or commit violence even when they know they will probably die in the ensuing retaliation. We shake our heads, wonder how they can so jeopardize their own lives, and then forget about them.

We can forget about them today because they can't seriously

threaten us with massive violence. They can commit acts of terror with machine guns or explosive devices, but only a small number of people are victimized. Even these incidents grip our attention while they are happening. But fortunately, almost none of us are at risk.

But what will happen, decades from now, when a new Khomeini, Qaddafi, Amin, or Pol Pot unveils several intercontinental ballistic missiles (ICBMs),[1] each armed with a nuclear, chemical, or biological warhead, aimed at an American city, and begins to make his demands and set his deadline? We will, of course, reply by saying, ''Your threat is suicidal. If you fire a single missile, we will destroy you in a devastating retaliation.'' Such a threat would surely deter us, if we were in his shoes. And it would no doubt deter the leaders of most nations. But can we be confident it will deter the heir of Khomeini, Qaddafi, Amin, or Pol Pot?

In the nuclear age, we have relied on the threat of devastating retaliation. We have deterred by threatening enormous punishment. Thus far, our strategy has worked. But we must face the fact that someday this may not deter the leader of the Nth country.

Suppose the heir to Khomeini orders us out of the Persian Gulf, or he will fire. Or the heir to Qaddafi makes the same threat about the Mediterranean? We will say, ''You can't be serious about firing. Don't you know what we will do to you if you fire? You must be crazy.'' But will we be able to sit tight until midnight, his firing deadline? Will we be willing to call his bluff when his missiles are aimed at our cities?

This Nth country leader of the future may be genuinely suicidal. He simply may not care what happens if he fires his missiles. Blinded by rage at our refusal to do what he wants, he may be ready to punish us, and then meet oblivion. Such people exist in the world today, but they don't yet have the power to truly hurt us. What if they acquire that power?

Nor will we be safe if the Nth country leader is merely a risk taker, rather than suicidal. Suppose he would only set a deadline if he thought we might capitulate. Can he think this? Do we know if we would ever capitulate? If we knew that our blackmailer would never actually fire, then of course we would stand firm. But could we be sure the heir to Khomeini, or Qaddafi, or Amin, or Pol Pot, won't fire if we refuse what he wants?

After all, his demand is probably something we can bear. Can we get out of the Persian Gulf, or the Mediterranean? Temporarily, of course we can. And he knows it. So even if he is not suicidal, but only a gambler, he may decide to make his demand and set his deadline. When the deadline is reached, if we fail to capitulate, his anger may rise. What if he gives the order to fire in an hour, and then boards a plane to escape before we retaliate?

So the stark question is this: What can we do to prepare for a threat by an Nth country that is willing to attempt nuclear, chemical, or biological blackmail despite our ability to retaliate?

Preparing for the Nth country threat

We must do everything possible to prevent any Nth country from acquiring ICBMs with nuclear, chemical, or biological warheads. The Soviets and other current nuclear powers should be willing to cooperate. After all, they too face the Nth country threat. The nuclear club expresses support, in theory, for nuclear nonproliferation. But in practice, proliferation of nuclear, chemical, and biological weapons, and of ballistic missile capability, creeps forward. Why?

One nation says, I only want reactors for peaceful purposes. Another says, I want missiles for the peaceful exploration of space. Another says, I'm building a chemical plant to supply medicines, not chemical weapons. Another says, I need a few bombs to deter an adversary who already belongs to the nuclear club. Another says, if you don't supply me, I'll become an ally of your adversary. Another says, if you don't sell it to me, I'll simply buy it from someone else. Another asks, why is it safe for you to have it, but not me? And there is no shortage of suppliers.

All of these arguments explain why proliferation continues. But we should acquiesce in none of them. The Nth country threat looms on the horizon. The clock is ticking. The realm of nuclear, chemical, and biological weapons and ballistic missiles is not the place to practice equality among nations. The fact is that the current nuclear club has the military, political, and economic power to slow nuclear, chemical, biological, and ballistic missile proliferation if it acts collectively and forcefully.

The United States has made diplomatic efforts to slow proliferation. But we must face the fact that decisive economic and military action will be necessary to keep nuclear, chemical, and biological weapons and ballistic missiles out of the hands of potentially dangerous adversaries. It is much nicer to discuss and negotiate. But we must accept the sad truth that an Nth country leader may emerge who cannot be persuaded, and who must be disarmed by the application of force.

What do we do if potentially dangerous facilities are under construction in an Nth country? We must seriously consider a preemptive attack on these facilities. Such an action will be difficult to take. Recall the world outcry against the Israeli attack on the Iraqi nuclear reactor in 1981. The Nth country will almost surely insist that its facilities are intended for peaceful, nonmilitary purposes. And it may be telling the truth. Thus far, neither the United States nor the Soviet Union has been willing to engage in this kind of preemptive attack on an Nth country.

So an Nth country may acquire facilities. Then it may secretly build, or acquire, ICBMs with nuclear, chemical, or biological warheads. What then? We must seriously consider a preemptive attack on the ICBMs before any blackmail has occurred. But even here, preemption is not easy. The Soviets have not done it with the Chinese. We rejected such preemption in Cuba in 1962, although we might have risked it if our naval blockade had failed. And if the missiles are already deployed, our attack itself may provoke a firing.

So what is our last resort? If the blackmailer fires his missiles, it would be nice to be able to shoot them down. But can an effective ballistic missile defense (BMD) be constructed at an acceptable cost? It is too early to know. Remember, we are not talking about a defense capable of handling a massive attack by today's Soviet offensive arsenal. Our problem regards an attack by an Nth country with a few ICBMs.

The debate that has raged since former President Reagan proposed his Strategic Defense Initiative (SDI) in 1983 is largely irrelevant to the issue at hand. Both the president and his critics focused almost exclusively on a ballistic missile defense aimed at the Soviet Union. Technical analyses of feasibility and cost have concentrated on the large Soviet offensive arsenal.

Our Nth country challenge is, fortunately, much less formidable. There is at least a reasonable chance that a defense against a small number of missiles can be constructed at a tolerable cost. Of course, no defense is guaranteed to be effective. But if the chance of success is high enough, and the cost low enough, it is worth acquiring. It is time for our BMD technical experts to redirect their energies, concentrate on the Nth country threat, and give us an assessment of technical feasibility and cost.[2]

Suppose we obtain such a defense. A suicidal Nth country leader may still make his demand and set his deadline, and when we don't capitulate, he may fire. But we will then have a very good chance of preventing any of his missiles from getting through. And the gambler who is not suicidal may not start his blackmail in the first place. Knowing we can shoot down his missiles, he will recognize that there is little chance we will capitulate, and a very high chance we will retaliate. Not being suicidal, he probably won't risk blackmail.

Of course, we must be ready to defend against an attack by aircraft as well as missiles, and there will always be the danger of the suitcase bomb smuggled into our country, or even a bomb assembled here by terrorists. But none of this alters the point that a ''population BMD''—a BMD that tries to protect our people— could be of vital necessity in the face of an Nth country threat. It could save millions of American lives.

Our initial BMD must be good enough to handle the offensive missiles now available to an Nth country. Unfortunately, we must be ready to gradually upgrade our BMD to keep pace with advances in Nth country offensive missiles. Alas, there is no way to negotiate with every potential Nth country and say, if you agree to use only a 1990 vintage of offense when you try to blackmail us, that would be nice, because then we only have to build a defense that can handle the 1990 vintage. I'm afraid we must be ready to upgrade our population defense gradually but indefinitely. This permanent "maintenance" cost should be included in any cost/benefit analysis of a BMD against an Nth country threat.

A population BMD, vital to guard against the Nth country threat, has another important benefit: it serves as accident insurance. So far we have been lucky in the nuclear age. No nation has launched a missile by mistake. Members of the current nuclear club have devised methods to reduce the chance of an accidental launch. For example, one method requires several persons to turn keys simultaneously to activate a missile, so that a single person cannot do it alone.

Experts assure us that the chance of an accidental launch is very small. So far so good. But accidents do happen. And the chance of an accident increases as proliferation spreads. It is simply foolish to go without accident insurance if it is available at a reasonable cost. Insurance means the ability of the launching nation, or target nation, to shoot down missiles in flight. For our safety, we want other nuclear powers to acquire the ability to destroy their own missiles in flight. Courtesy surely requires that we be able to do the same. But since they may not do this, our best accident insurance policy may be a population BMD.[3]

Although we have watched the trouble spots of the world on many an evening news, we are at this moment completely defenseless against an Nth country missile attack or an accidental launch. Are we sure that technical unfeasibility or prohibitive cost require us to remain this way? Decades from now, what will we say to our children or grandchildren as a few Nth country missiles begin their descent? Will we tell them there was nothing we could do? Will our last words to them be the truth?

Deterring the Soviet Union

Let us now turn to the problem of deterring the Soviet Union. The Soviets have been a tough adversary since the end of World War II. They have dominated the nations of Eastern Europe. They ruthlessly suppressed uprisings in Hungary in 1956, Czechoslovakia in 1968, and Poland in the 1980s. They repeatedly threatened West Berlin until 1961, when they built the Berlin Wall. They fought a brutal war for nearly a decade in an attempt to control Afghanistan. They have probed for advantage in places like Cuba, Nicaragua, the horn of Africa, and Angola. They have imprisoned their own dissidents and limited emigration. Whether the new Gorbachev regime will change Soviet foreign policy fundamentally remains to be seen.

Nevertheless, even before Gorbachev, the Soviet leadership has usually avoided unnecessary risk-taking.[4] They have not attempted a preemptive strike at Chinese ICBMs. They have refrained from using nuclear weapons in Afghanistan, just as we refrained in Korea and Vietnam, even though they have been unable to defeat the Afghan rebels. Since 1962, they have generally avoided provocations that would create a serious nuclear crisis with the United States. In contrast to our Nth country leader of the future, the Soviet leaders appear risk-averse. They are unlikely to take unnecessary aggressive actions that have even a small chance of provoking a U.S. nuclear retaliation. Thus, as long as Soviet leaders know their nation is targeted by invulnerable U.S. weapons, they are likely to probe cautiously.

So we must simultaneously pursue two objectives in our defense planning. We must prepare for the Nth country threat, where our readiness to retaliate may be insufficient, and a population defense may be technically feasible and affordable. And we must deter the Soviet leaders by continuing to hold their nation vulnerable to our retaliation.

A crucial implication follows from our two goals. If we build a BMD aimed at an Nth country threat, and gradually upgrade it to stay ahead of the Nth country advances, no doubt the Soviets will do the same. But to keep the Soviets at risk, we must gradually increase our retaliatory capacity, so that the Kremlin knows it remains vulnerable despite the upgrading of the Soviet population defense.

A small-scale population BMD that is just good enough to handle the Nth country threat or an accidental launch will be no match for current U.S. or Soviet offensive arsenals. If these

BMDs are initially introduced, neither we nor the Soviets will need to adjust our offensive arsenals to assure the ability to penetrate. Eventually, as we each gradually upgrade our BMDs to stay ahead of the Nth country, we will need to gradually upgrade our offensive arsenals in order to preserve our ability to penetrate.

But how can we and the Soviets know that our defenses are modest, aimed only at Nth countries and accidents? Quite easily. Although offensive missiles can be readily hidden in forests or under oceans, a nationwide BMD is easy to detect and assess. Can the Soviets be sure we are not planning a sudden dramatic upgrading of our defense? Of course. They need only follow Congressional debates and read our newspapers. True, we must rely on our intelligence services, rather than Soviet media, but we too should have no trouble learning of a planned "breakout," and keeping our offensive arsenal ahead of it should it occur.

Note also that it is not our relation with the Soviets that prevents a limit to this gradual escalation of defense and retaliatory capacity. If we and the Soviets were the only two nations on earth, we might limit population defense permanently, and acquire only enough retaliatory capacity to hold each other at risk. Instead, it is the gradual improvement in the Nth country's offensive potential that drives the escalation. Unfortunately, in a world where proliferation can be slowed but not stopped, there is no safe way to escape it.

Crisis stability[5] with the Soviets

When are we safer? When we and the Soviets each have a thousand missiles with a thousand nuclear warheads, or just ten missiles with ten warheads?

Suppose the thousand missiles are based on two hundred small submarines—five per sub—scattered and hidden under the vast oceans. Assume neither side can locate the other's subs. If we strike first against the Soviet homeland, its subs will be unscathed, ready to launch a devastating retaliatory strike against our homeland. And if they strike first against our homeland, our subs will all survive, ready to devastate the Soviet Union. We each know this. And we each know that the other knows it too.

So in a crisis, with a thousand invulnerable submarine-based missiles on each side, both sides may as well wait. There is nothing to be gained by striking first at the other side's homeland. Go first, and you will suffer as much devastation as if you go second. Going first gains you nothing, because your first strike does no damage to your adversary's retaliatory weapons, which are safely hidden on submarines you cannot hit. With a thousand submarine-based missiles on each side, the odds are very high that both sides will wait, and the crisis will eventually be resolved without a nuclear war.

But now imagine that each side has ten highly accurate land-based missiles in "soft" (vulnerable) fixed silos, and that each side knows the location of the other side's ten missiles. Assume that whichever side fires first will destroy the other side's ten missiles in their silos, and therefore suffer no casualties. Suddenly, a serious crisis develops with the Soviet Union, and you are called to the oval office to advise the president.

Everyone wants to resolve the crisis without firing the missiles. But one adviser points out: "Mr. President, if we wait, and the Soviets strike first, millions of Americans will die, and we will be unable to retaliate. And the Kremlin knows it. But if we strike first, we can take out all their missiles, and no Americans will die. The Kremlin also knows this. And they are meeting at this very moment. They may fire any minute. Mr. President, please give the order to fire immediately, and save millions of American lives."

What would you advise? I'm sure you are horrified about firing missiles that, although aimed at their ten missiles, will inevitably kill millions of innocent Soviet civilians. On the other hand, your own children's lives are at stake. Make up your mind now. The decision must be made instantly.

Whatever your decision, I'm sure you will agree that there is a frighteningly high chance that either the Kremlin, the White

House, or both, will give the order to fire. Is there any doubt that the chance of nuclear war is much greater if each side has ten vulnerable, accurate, land-based missiles than if each side has a thousand invulnerable submarine-based missiles?

I'm sure everyone would agree that we don't want our missiles vulnerable to a first strike by the Soviets. We don't want the Kremlin to think it can take out our missiles if it strikes first. But do we want the Soviets to hide their missiles from us? How should we regard the news that they are switching from fixed land-based missiles we can locate and hit, to mobile land-based missiles or submarine-based missiles we cannot locate or hit? Should we react with alarm? Many citizens do when they read such reports.

But the same logic says we should react with relief. If they know their missiles are invulnerable, they can afford to wait in a crisis. No longer will we have any temptation to strike first to save American lives, because we cannot take out their missiles with a first strike. And they will no longer be under pressure to "use 'em or lose 'em." So when they hide their missiles, we are safer.

While everyone will agree that we don't want the Soviets to develop highly accurate missiles, what about us? Is it good for us to develop enough accurate missiles to target all their land-based missiles? It might be worth having a few invulnerable, highly accurate missiles targeted on the bunkers of the Soviet leaders. But, should they be foolish enough to leave their missiles exposed, do we want enough accurate missiles to target all of their missiles? No. Because in a crisis we would then be tempted to strike first to save American lives. And recognizing this, they would be under pressure to "use 'em or lose 'em." For the same reason that we want them to hide their missiles, we don't want to deploy many accurate missiles of our own.

Suppose we can't hide all our missiles. Would it be desirable to protect our exposed missiles from attack by encircling them with a ballistic missile defense (BMD) that can shoot down attacking missiles?[6] Yes, provided the cost is acceptable, because protecting our missiles has the same effect as hiding them. It enhances our ability to retaliate against a Soviet first strike.

But should we want the Soviets to ring their exposed missiles with a BMD that can shoot down our attacking missiles? Yes. We not only want them to hide their missiles, but to protect them as well. Then we will not be tempted to strike first to save American lives. And recognizing this, they will not feel pressure to "use 'em or lose 'em."

We have already concluded that we may want to develop a population BMD to guard against the Nth country threat and an accidental launch. But how would such a population defense affect crisis stability with the Soviets? It is often argued that a population defense is destabilizing. Why?

The argument goes like this. Our population BMD will not be good enough to handle a Soviet first strike, but it may be good enough to handle a Soviet retaliation if our first strike destroys enough Soviet weapons. So in a crisis we may be tempted to strike first to save American lives. And anticipating this, the Soviets will feel pressure to use theirs first.

But the key step in this argument is the assumption that our first strike can destroy enough Soviet weapons to make a difference. If the Soviets hide most of their weapons under the oceans or on land, or protect them with hardening or a BMD, then their second strike will be almost as powerful as a first strike. Despite our defense, going first will gain us little, so our defense will not tempt us to strike first to save American lives. Knowing this, the Soviets will not feel pressure to strike first. So if the Soviets make most of their weapons invulnerable to our first strike, then our population defense will not tempt either of us to go first in a crisis.

Population defenses will not reduce crisis stability as long as both sides keep sufficient retaliatory weapons invulnerable. That way, each side will know that it gains little from going first, because its population defense is not much better at handling a second strike than a first strike. So if we both prepare for the Nth country threat and an accidental launch by upgrading BMD population defenses, it is crucial that we both keep most of our retaliatory weapons invulnerable.

Let's summarize. If cost were no constraint, what advice would we give each side?

Keep your retaliatory weapons invulnerable. Hide them. One good place is under the oceans. Don't put all your retaliatory eggs in a few submarine baskets, just in case the other side tries to track you. Scatter your missiles in many small submarines. Another way to hide missiles is to keep them on land, but make them mobile. Move them on trucks or trains, or conceal them in forests. Harden the silos of land-based missiles. Protect land-based missile, bomber, and submarine bases with a ballistic missile defense (BMD) that shoots down attacking missiles.

Diversify your retaliatory portfolio. Preserve your "triad" of submarine-based missiles, land-based missiles, and bombers, so that if the other side finds a way to take out one in a first strike, two others will remain. The triad is like a multiengined airplane. When one engine breaks down, the plane keeps flying. Don't try to fly on a single engine.

Don't eliminate any part of your triad. It may seem nice to abolish all missiles, but if one side finds a way to surprise attack the other side's bomber bases, it may be tempted to strike first in a crisis. Or it may seem nice to abolish land-based missiles and bombers, and rely solely on subs, but if one side finds a way to track and hit subs, it might be tempted to strike first in a crisis.

Don't threaten most of the other side's weapons. Don't pursue first-strike capability. It's all right to acquire a few highly accurate invulnerable missiles to target the adversary's political leadership. But don't acquire enough accurate missiles to severely threaten any leg of your adversary's triad.

Limit your own ability to execute a "prompt" surprise attack. Rely more heavily on weapons that take hours, rather than minutes, to strike. Slow weapons can retaliate with as much devastation as fast weapons, but they cannot execute a surprise first strike. Thus, rely more on slow-flying cruise missiles and bombers, and less on fast-flying ballistic missiles. Keep your submarines with nuclear missiles far from your adversary's shores, thereby reducing his fear that you will attempt a surprise attack.

Now some of these stabilizing steps would be very expensive, so it may not be worth taking all of them. Specialists must assess the best way to allocate funds in order to maximize crisis stability. For example, if each of the following have the same cost, specialists must decide which contributes most to crisis stability: x mobile land-based missiles, a BMD of capability y that protects missile and bomber bases, or z small subs. My central point is simply that these tough choices should be made with a clear goal in mind: the enhancement of crisis stability.

To implore, match, or offset

This advice is all very nice, but there is one little problem. What if the Soviets ignore it? What if the Soviets appear determined to acquire first-strike capability—enough highly accurate weapons and population defense to tempt them to strike first in a crisis, and make us feel pressure to "use 'em or lose 'em"?

We can implore the Soviets not to pursue first-strike capability. We can say: "You're crazy to build so many accurate missiles. Don't you understand our analysis? You will reduce your own safety, because you will be tempted to strike in a crisis to save lives on your side, and we will be under pressure to 'use 'em or lose 'em,' so we will also be more likely to strike." Our imploring strategy may work. It is possible that the Soviets will be won over to our analysis. Then again, they may not. If not, and all we do is implore, they will achieve first-strike capability and we won't. According to our analysis, this makes us both more likely to strike in a crisis. According to their analysis, whatever it is, they will believe they are now in a position to intimidate us, and we should recognize that we must yield when they make demands. So if our imploring falls on deaf ears, the outcome may be quite dangerous.

Instead of imploring, we can pledge to match the Soviets. We can say: "All right, if you're going to pursue first-strike capability, so will we. If you acquire enough accurate weapons and population defense to create pressure to go first in a crisis, we will acquire enough accurate weapons and population defense to create still more pressure to go first.'' By threatening to match them, we hope they will agree to give up their quest.

Our matching strategy may work. It will work if the Soviets would rather do without first-strike capability than see us acquire it. But what if they prefer to acquire first-strike capability even if we will match it? Then our matching strategy will backfire. We will end up with a large arsenal of accurate weapons, and a population defense, and so will they. In a crisis, each will be under great pressure to strike first in order to save lives on its side.

A better strategy is to commit publicly to offset. We should say: ''If you try to obtain first-strike capability, we will thwart you. If you try to target all our land-based missiles, we will build mobile ones and protect them with a BMD. If you try to track all our subs, we will build more, and will improve their deception. If you build a defense to protect yourself against our retaliation, we will improve our ability to penetrate your defense. We will do whatever is necessary to prevent you from achieving first-strike capability.''

This is a better strategy because it guarantees that the Soviets will not achieve first-strike capability. Of course, if they don't believe we will stick to it, we may both waste a lot of money as they build first-strike weapons and defenses, and we offset them. But crisis stability will be preserved.

However, if we convince them, through actual acquisition and deployment, that we really will spend whatever it takes to offset them, then why should they continue their quest? With our economy twice as productive as theirs, they certainly don't want a cost race for its own sake. So there is a good chance that our public commitment to offset will prevent a cost race. Then we will preserve crisis stability without such a race.

To obtain this best of all outcomes, we must show, through deed as well as word, that we will spend whatever it takes to thwart them. We must show them that we will offset, not merely implore.

It should now be evident that a simpleminded aversion to spending more on weapons, regardless of what the Soviets do, is dangerous. It may result in the Soviets' obtaining first-strike capability. If a citizen really wants neither side to have such a capability, then he should support a commitment to offset. Such a commitment means a willingness to spend whatever is necessary to preserve our ability to retaliate.

Lessons for arms control agreements

We do not need signed agreements in order to follow the advice just given. Without agreements, we can preserve our ability to retaliate no matter what offense or defense the Soviets attempt, and we can refrain from acquiring first-strike capability. We can inform the Soviets that they will waste their money if they try to obtain first-strike capability, and we can prove it with spending deeds. Thus, unilaterally, we can prevent their obtaining first-strike capability. At the same time, we can show them, by the weapons we don't acquire, that we are not pursuing first-strike capability.

But wouldn't it be better to solidify our mutual commitment in signed agreements? Generally, no, and I'll explain why.

Any agreement worth signing must be verifiable. Otherwise, each side will fear that the other is secretly violating the agreement, and the result will be a heightening of tensions and suspicion. Consider an agreement to place a ceiling on the number of missiles. Verification requires location of the other side's missiles so that they can be counted. But remember our advice to each side: Hide your weapons so that they are safe from a first strike. How can this advice to conceal be harmonized with the need to locate in order to count and verify? The answer is that it cannot. So which is more important: concealment to assure the ability to retaliate, or a verifiable signed agreement?[7]

Consider an example. Suppose we sign an agreement with the

Soviets that limits each side to possessing only ten land-based missiles. To make it verifiable, each side must tell the other the location of its ten missiles so that periodic counting can occur. But in a crisis, each side will know where to aim its missiles, and each may then hope to prevent the other's retaliation by striking first.

Suppose, instead, we say to the Soviets informally, "We will hide a substantial number of missiles on a large number of small subs under the oceans far from your shores, and we urge you to do the same. We won't tell you how many we have, or where they are, and we don't want or expect you to tell us how many you have or where they are."

If we both do this, then in a crisis, each side will know that it cannot prevent massive retaliation if it strikes first. By contrast, under the formal verifiable agreement limiting each country to just ten land-based missiles, each side would be tempted to strike first in a crisis. Is there any doubt which situation is safer and more desirable?

So a signed agreement has a fatal flaw. If it is not verifiable, then each side will fear that the other is secretly violating it, and will in turn be tempted to cheat. If either side catches the other cheating, this in itself may provoke a crisis. On the other hand, if it is verifiable, then location and counting undermine each side's assured second-strike capability.

Aren't there any agreements worth signing? Consider an agreement for ocean zones. In our informal discussion with the Soviets, we said we would keep our subs far from their shores, to reduce our ability to execute a surprise attack. Why not sign an agreement that restricts U.S. subs to a zone far from the Soviet Union, and Soviet subs to a zone far from the United States? Each would patrol its own zone to detect any intrusion by its adversary. It is possible that the chance of detection would be high enough to deter cheating.

But the problem is that subs are needed for conventional as well as nuclear missions. Since these missions require, for example, our access to the Mediterranean Sea or the Persian Gulf, we cannot agree to avoid these waters. Of course, we can promise that these subs won't have nuclear weapons, but why should the Soviets believe us?

What about an agreement limiting only highly accurate missiles? These are often called first-strike weapons. The problem is that we may want a few accurate weapons to threaten retaliation against the Soviet leadership, or perhaps an Nth country leadership. Any verifiable agreement will require us to give the Soviets the location of our accurate missiles. But then, in a crisis, the Soviets may be tempted to strike first at these known locations.

It would be safer to try to restrain highly accurate missiles without a signed agreement. With no agreement, we are free to hide a few accurate missiles to target the Soviet leadership. Informally, we should tell the Soviets that their quest for first-strike capability is futile. By spending deeds, we may be able to convince them that there is no point wasting their money. Even if we can't convince them, our offsetting will prevent their first-strike capability, and their leaders will never doubt our ability to retaliate. But if we do persuade them that their quest is futile, then both sides can reach a tacit understanding to slow the acquisition of accurate missiles without a formal agreement.

It's too bad that we have to worry about the Nth country threat and an accidental launch, because otherwise an agreement prohibiting a nationwide population BMD, like the ABM Treaty of 1972, would be attractive. While we are probably unable to know how many missiles the Soviets are hiding on subs or in forests, we can easily tell whether they are deploying a nationwide population BMD. In this case, verification is feasible, and it enhances crisis stability. While we don't want each side to know the location of the other side's missiles, we do want each to know whether the other has deployed an ambitious population BMD.

But we and the Soviets may want to prepare for an Nth country threat and an accidental launch by gradually upgrading BMD population defenses. Of course, we should try to reassure each other that the defenses are aimed only at the Nth country and an accidental launch. But what we say to each other doesn't matter much. The fact is that each side will assess the other's defenses, and then upgrade its offense so that it can still penetrate in a retaliation.

So we must liberate ourselves from our fixation with signed agreements. In certain circumstances, a signed agreement may be desirable—for example, with nuclear testing in the atmosphere. But generally, a signed agreement will be harmful, because verification requires counting and locating, and counting and locating jeopardize the ability to retaliate.

Should we sign a radical reduction agreement with the Soviet Union?

Thus far we have assumed that we must preserve our ability to retaliate against the Soviet leadership. But let's reconsider. Maybe we and the Soviets should give up the ability to retaliate. Why don't we both upgrade our population defenses, and sign an agreement to radically reduce our offensive weapons, so that neither side retains the ability to retaliate effectively? It would be nice to think that the Soviets can no longer devastate us. An agreement to drastically cut offensive weapons would eliminate the ability of either side to destroy the other in a retaliation, provided both sides comply. Trying to count and locate weapons would no longer be counterproductive, because neither side would seek to protect its ability to retaliate. We might sleep better at night under such a signed agreement.

Or would we? Suppose the Soviets cheat, and secretly develop offensive weapons that can penetrate our defense. After all, can we really verify that in the vast reaches of the Soviet Union there will be no factories turning out new missiles and weapons? Can we really be confident they will be unable to hide these new missiles in their forests, or under the ocean? Remember, we are not talking about verifying whether they are testing new weapons by exploding them in the atmosphere, or deploying a nationwide BMD, but about whether they are producing and hiding missiles and warheads.

If they cheat, then at the right moment, the Soviets could

display their new offense, which they would no doubt justify as a response to our alleged cheating, and make demands from behind their defense. This situation would be more dangerous for us than the situation that has prevailed since the end of World War II, where Soviet leaders have been constrained by their recognition that we can retaliate.

So if we sign an agreement cutting weapons, we may be safer if the Soviets comply and are internationally docile, but in deep trouble if the Soviets cheat and are internationally aggressive. Should we take the chance? A Kremlin with a desire to bully us would surely cheat. But even a Kremlin with no desire to bully us might cheat simply because it fears we are secretly cheating. So could we afford not to cheat? And if we must cheat to remain safe, why sign such an agreement in the first place?

Moreover, we may not be able to successfully cheat. Our free press, and those citizens who support the reduction agreement, would monitor our compliance. Our cheating would probably be discovered, producing bitter domestic division, and undermining our credibility abroad. So if we sign a reduction agreement, our government may really abide by it.

The Kremlin, of course, will not have to worry about a free press, or its own citizens, monitoring compliance. So a simple question arises: Why subject ourselves to this asymmetry? Why sign an agreement that the Soviets may be able to violate, but we may have to obey?

Ironically, under a signed radical reduction agreement, Soviet-American relations would almost surely become much more tense, suspicious, and dangerous than they are today. For today, we both know each can retaliate, and there is little danger that tomorrow one side will surprise the other by removing its ability to retaliate. So each has a self-confidence that does not depend on trusting the other.

But under a radical reduction agreement, each will be nervous that the other is cheating. Each knows that, on any given day, one may announce it has secretly acquired the ability to penetrate the other's defense. Rumors will be rife on both sides. The slightest friction in a negotiating session will bring fears that the other side is about to announce a "breakout" from the reduction agreement.

Even today, one suspicious facility in the Soviet heartland has caused some of our citizens to fear that the Soviets are about to "break out" of the ABM Treaty of 1972 and deploy a nationwide BMD. But at least there is no doubt that we can detect the facilities needed to deploy such a BMD. Imagine the situation when our concern is whether they are producing missiles and warheads in a secluded factory, and hiding them in forests or on submarines? How could we ever be sure there are no such factories, and that missiles aren't being hidden?

Unfortunately, then, signing a radical reduction agreement would be a mistake. Does this mean we are condemned to a hostile, unrestrained race with the Soviets to accumulate offensive weapons? Not at all.

We should seek a tacit understanding with the Soviets. Informally, we should tell them, "We are upgrading our limited population defense to guard against an Nth country or an accidental launch, and improving our retaliatory capacity to preserve our ability to penetrate your defense. We will not seek a first-strike capability, and if you do, we will thwart you."

Then we should back our words with deeds. We should restrain our acquisition of accurate weapons so that we obtain only enough to target the Soviet leadership, but not nearly enough to execute a first strike on all Soviet weapons. And we should promptly respond to any Soviet buildup of accurate weapons by producing more invulnerable weapons.

This informal approach has a good chance of inducing reciprocal behavior by the Soviets. Neither side needs to trust the other. Each can observe the gradual upgrading of the other's limited population defense, and assess what it needs to penetrate it. Each can estimate how many invulnerable weapons it needs to assure its ability to retaliate. By preserving its triad, and keeping plenty of extra margin in its ability to retaliate, each can relax about its inability to know exactly how many weapons the other side is building and hiding.

Under this tacit mutual understanding, there is little chance that one side will surprise the other. And each side knows it. Small frictions in relations will not generate sudden fear of cheating, vulnerability, and suspicion, as they would under a radical reduction agreement. Rumors would result in mild concern, not sudden panic. Each side would know it has plenty of time to respond to any new development by the other.

Should we sign an abolition agreement?

The case against an abolition agreement is even stronger than the case against a radical reduction agreement with the Soviets, for one simple reason. Under an agreement abolishing nuclear weapons, we would not only be vulnerable to Soviet cheating, but also to Nth country cheating.

Sometime in the future, an Nth country leader will be tempted to obtain a few missiles with nuclear, chemical, or biological warheads from a secret supplier, or from his own technicians. Will he do it? If he's suicidal, he won't hesitate, even if we have an adequate population BMD, and can retaliate with nuclear weapons.

But suppose he's merely a risk taker. Our BMD may discourage him, but there is still a small chance we may meet any demands he makes. After all, we can't be absolutely confident of our BMD.

Then he may ask the key question: Will the United States retaliate with nuclear weapons if I attempt blackmail? If the answer is no, he may try it. If the answer is yes, or even maybe, he may not.

So our question must be: How will our signature on an abolition agreement affect a future Nth country leader? If he's suicidal, he will go ahead even if we were armed to the teeth. And if he's cautious, he won't try blackmail even if we've given up our nuclear weapons. But if he's a risk taker, our abolition just may make the difference. If we have no nuclear weapons, he may decide to take a chance.

But wouldn't an abolition agreement make it more difficult for the Nth country leader to obtain missiles and nuclear weapons? Not at all. In fact, it would probably make it easier. If we and many other nations abolish our nuclear weapons, some Nth country leaders will see a new opportunity for blackmail. They will become more eager to obtain weapons, and more willing to pay a higher price. A higher price will call forth secret suppliers.

What must be grasped is that we can work aggressively to slow proliferation without signing an abolition agreement, and that proliferation can accelerate even if we sign an abolition agreement. True, some leaders will be inspired by our example, and will abolish their weapons because we do. But will the inspired include the heirs of Khomeini, Qaddafi, Amin, and Pol Pot?

A cynic may advise, sign the abolition agreement, but then cheat on it. This is bad advice. First, all that matters is what the Nth country leader thinks. If he thinks we're weaponless, then he may try blackmail. We'll resist, but he may fire, and we can never be sure our BMD will be completely effective.

Moreover, we probably won't be able to conceal our cheating because our free press and our citizens who support the abolition agreement will monitor our compliance. So if we sign an abolition agreement, we will probably have to abide by it. But others won't. Many nations do not have a press or citizenry able to monitor compliance. So, as in the case of a radical reduction agreement with the Soviets, a simple question arises: Why subject ourselves to asymmetry? Why sign an agreement that others will ignore, but we will probably have to obey? After all, we are not talking about an abolition agreement in a world with three countries—the United States, Britain, and Canada. We live in a world with over a hundred nations, many with totalitarian governments, some who fervently hate us, and some with leaders who would be insulted to learn that I named Khomeini and Qaddafi, and not them.

Unfortunately, in the real world, with the Nth country threat looming on the horizon, signing an abolition agreement would be a dangerous mistake. The maximum protection against the Nth country threat requires both a population BMD and the ability to retaliate with nuclear weapons. Should we take a chance and face the Nth country threat with only one?

Sober realism

We live in a dangerous world, and it will grow more dangerous. The Nth country threat cannot be wished away, and we ignore it at our peril. Unfortunately, the other most powerful nation has been a tough adversary, and it is too early to know whether its new regime will enable a permanent reduction in tension.

Our challenge is to adopt an attitude of sober realism. We must prepare for an Nth country nuclear blackmail attempt, or an accidental launch, and build a small-scale population defense, provided it is technically feasible at an acceptable cost. We must deter the Soviets by continuing to hold them vulnerable to a U.S. retaliation. At the same time, we and the Soviets must keep our retaliatory weapons hidden or protected, so that neither side has anything to gain by striking first in a crisis.

We should generally avoid formal agreements on offensive weapons, because they suffer from a fatal flaw: verification requires locating, but locating tempts each side to strike first in a crisis. Besides, how can we be sure that missiles are not being produced in a secluded factory, and being hidden in forests or beneath the ocean? A radical cut in weapons would release the Soviets from vulnerability to a U.S. retaliation, and an abolition agreement would also release Nth country leaders. So we should sign neither agreement.

Instead, we should seek an informal, tacit understanding with the Soviets. We should cooperate to slow proliferation. We should build population defenses to handle the Nth country threat or an accidental launch, and acquire sufficient invulnerable weapons to preserve our ability to retaliate. We should not seek first-strike capability, and we should show the Soviets that we will thwart them if they do.

This approach is not dramatic. It does not eliminate all danger.

It offers nothing as exciting as the signing of an abolition agreement, or even a radical reduction agreement. But in a dangerous world—the world as it really is, not as we would like it to be—this approach is the least dangerous course.

Notes

1. The spread of ballistic missile capability among Nth countries is documented by Aaron Karp in "Ballistic Missiles in the Third World," *International Security* 9 (Winter 1984–85), 166–95, and in "The Frantic Third World Quest for Ballistic Missiles," *Bulletin of the Atomic Scientists* 44 (June 1988), 14–20, where Karp writes: "These events illustrate that ballistic missiles are becoming an ominous reality in the Third World. Indeed, 20 Third World countries, including Israel and Brazil, currently possess ballistic missiles or are striving to develop them" (p. 14). Thus far, these missiles generally have a range suitable only for regional conflict.

2. The misallocation of expert energies in the 1980s is illustrated by the fact that there are many published technical studies and cost estimates of a defense aimed at the Soviet arsenal, but few of a defense aimed at an Nth country threat.

3. Senator Sam Nunn, chairman of the Senate Armed Services Committee, has proposed serious consideration of a limited BMD with this objective in mind. It is called the "Accidental Launch Protection System" (ALPS), which he describes in his article, "Arms Control in the Last Year of the Reagan Administration," in *Arms Control Today* 18 (March 1988), 3–7. Nunn wants an assessment of technical feasibility and cost before proceeding to construction. In the April 1988 issue of the *Bulletin of the Atomic Scientists* 44, a journal that has strongly opposed an SDI against the Soviet Union, contributing editor Michael Krepon writes: "Nunn's centrist alternative to grandiose SDI deployment schemes will require a delicate balancing act between ardent supporters and critics of arms control. It will take time to sort out the technical capabilities and costs of his proposed accidental launch protection system. Nevertheless, a careful assessment of ALPS's pros and cons should be high on the next president's agenda" (p. 5).

4. Khrushchev's attempt to install missiles in Cuba in 1962 appears to be an exception.

5. This analysis of crisis stability is based on a large literature which includes: Thomas Schelling, "Surprise Attack and Disarmament," in his *The Strategy of Conflict* (Cambridge, Mass.: Harvard University Press, 1960) pp. 230–54. D. Ellsberg, "The Crude Analysis of Strategic Choices," *American Economic Review Papers and Proceedings* 51 (May 1961): 472–78; M. Nicholson, "Uncertainty and Crisis Behavior: An Illustration of Conflict," in C. Carter and J. Ford, eds., *Uncertainty and Expectations in Economics* (Fair-

field, N.J.: Augustus M. Kelley Publishers, 1972); C. Glaser, "Why Even Good Defenses May Be Bad," *International Security* 9 (Fall 1984): 92–123; S. Brams, *Superpower Games* (New Haven: Yale University Press, 1985); B. O'Neill, "A Measure for Crisis Instability with an Application to Space-Based Antimissile Systems," *Journal of Conflict Resolution* 31 (December 1987); L. Seidman, "Crisis Stability," *Journal of Conflict Resolution* (forthcoming 1990).

    6. Note that this BMD tries to protect our missiles against a Soviet attack, in contrast to the BMD discussed earlier, which tries to protect our population against an Nth country attack. Each BMD should be subject to its own cost/benefit analysis.

    7. This important point is emphasized by Thomas Schelling in "What Went Wrong With Arms Control?" *Foreign Affairs* 64 (Winter 1985-86), 219–33, and Charles Krauthammer, "The End of Arms Control," *The New Republic*, 29 August 1988, 26–31.

ABOUT THE AUTHOR

Laurence S. Seidman is Associate Professor of Economics at the University of Delaware. He has published scholarly articles in a wide range of journals and has written a college text, *Macrodynamics* (Harcourt Brace Jovanovich, 1987).